Journey to hEALING *praise*

There are no rulebooks or manuals that come with your child when they are born, and there is no rulebook or manual that you receive when your child dies.

We navigate this new world without our child by making the rules as we go, or we learn from others who have walked this path before us.

Journey to HEALING serves as a testament of someone who is living and teaching others how to navigate this new world. It is a book based on healing, peace, and living a life with joy and love after a tragedy. *Journey to HEALING* is a definite must for those grieving as part of an arsenal of tools needed to survive and thrive after the death of a child.

~Wanda Campbell

Finding the right book about child loss is crucial when your child dies. *Journey to HEALING* will help you navigate the pain, to find hope and healing.

~Jill Townshend Lee

As a bereaved mom, I am able to relate to everything outlined in *Journey to HEALING* and found myself saying; *I know exactly what you mean,* as I read. Lisa provides helpful suggestions for coping with the devastation that accompanies the loss of a child. Her perspective, shared with the stories and wisdom of other mothers validated my feelings and allowed me to realize I was not alone. The suggestions in this book are simple and straightforward. If you've lost a child, this is a companion that you need.

~Melanie Delorme

Journey to HEALING

A Mother's Guide
to
Navigating Child Loss

*Together
we are stronger
xo Lisa
Boehm*

LISA K. BOEHM

Printed in the United States of America

Published by Author Academy Elite
P.O. Box 43, Powell, OH 43035
AuthorAcademyElite.com

Paperback ISBN: 978-1-64085-504-5
Hardback ISBN: 978-1-64085-505-2
Ebook ISBN: 978-1-64085-506-9

Library of Congress Control Number: 2018913833

For Katie,

Because of you,
I believe in angels.

The Gift of a Story

This book was born from a short story I wrote one afternoon in a matter of minutes. It flowed so freely from my heart that it might have been gifted to me as a message to share with others. However, this story sat on my laptop and in my heart for almost a year before I realized it was a bridge to something bigger–*Journey to HEALING*.

Stories touch us, they teach us, and they help us understand. They are the way we connect emotionally and they help us gain insight and find strength.

I knew from the start that *Journey to HEALING* would contain stories, experiences, and words from other bereaved mothers as well as my own. It was never an option. I knew I wanted to share their words and children with you. There is power in every anecdote and I am honoured that they were entrusted to me.

Journey to HEALING suggests helpful strategies to navigate the lonely and difficult road of child loss. But it's also about a surprising discovery, like the short story below. Within the devastation of loss there is beauty, and within the anguish is love. When you open yourself up to this, you will find comfort and peace. This takes time and effort, but it is possible.

The story that follows is the foundation of this book. I invite you to start here and know that you do not walk alone on this journey.

The Suitcase

One night a man came to my door. He gave me a suitcase that I had never seen before. Although he carefully placed it in my hands, it was too heavy and awkward to hold. It was heavy, black, and burdensome. It was broken and beat up.

The suitcase was difficult to deal with. I had never been given anything like it. Not knowing what to do with the suitcase, I started carrying it everywhere with me. I was afraid to set it down, afraid the secrets it carried would be lost forever.

People looked at my bag and felt sorry for me. Why had I been stuck with such a burden? They all secretly thought, "Thank goodness I don't have to carry that."

Days turned into weeks and I finally opened up the heavy, broken suitcase just a crack. Without enough light to shine in, it still appeared black and dark inside. The inside seemed as dark as the outside so I closed it up again.

Despite the heavy suitcase, I got stronger since I carried it everywhere I went. People commented on my strength.

They said, "I don't know how you do it." The fact was I didn't know either.

One day, I opened it up fully. Once I trusted myself with the heaviness, the brightness from inside began to shine outward. Inside the suitcase all this time was love, light, and all things beautiful. It contained treasures and memories that made me smile.

You see, the night I was told my daughter died was the night I began carrying my big, ugly bag of grief. On the outside grief was heavy, dark, and hideous. It hurt to carry it, sleep with it, and exist with it. I struggled to breathe as it lay upon my chest.

But when I took a look inside my grief, I saw what was there all along—love. The intense grief was a sign of all the love inside. Once I saw the love and memories of my beautiful daughter the more I was able to handle the ugly exterior.

The suitcase has not gotten any lighter or any less dark and ugly. However, the beautiful interior encourages me to open it up regularly to enjoy the love, beauty, and meaning inside. I now know that grief exists because love exists and I will continue living with my suitcase firmly in my hand because of what it represents—the memories of 17½ wonderful years.

Together we are Stronger

My daughter's fatal car accident changed my life. It ended the life that I knew and forced me to start a new one. The problem was I didn't know how. I had met bereaved mothers who seemed stuck in their grief, who let their grief define them and that scared me. I needed to find a way to navigate my grief that wouldn't destroy my son, my marriage, or me. I was determined to find a way to endure the indescribable pain.

On this road I now walk, I have found peace. I have found peace because I learned to live with love in my heart instead of fear, guilt, blame, and anger. I found a way to build my life *around* my grief and pain, not the other way around. I even found a way to smile and be grateful for the time I had with my daughter. Finding peace and accepting a new life takes work. A lot of work. But it can be done.

As I staggered and stumbled along my path, I pleaded with the universe, "Just tell me what to do!" I found lots of books about grief and child loss but I wanted simple, straightforward, helpful advice. I wanted someone to tell me how to survive my new reality. I wanted tips and strategies—concrete and tangible actions.

Over time, I have learned to navigate the pain and grief; how to live and find hope on the darkest days. *Journey to HEALING* comes from love and the desire to help others who walk this path. Within this book, I share everything that has helped me.

My healing also comes from the courageous mothers I have met along the way. These mothers are angel moms and they are survivors. They have held me up from the start and inspired me to keep going. I looked to these extraordinary souls for strength and support. I asked some of these women to share their experiences and wisdom with me. They provided interviews, personal essays and shared insightful social media posts that will fill you with hope. Their stories of strength and words of inspiration are woven into *Journey to HEALING*.

I had no idea how much this project would impact me. Each story was filled with heartbreak, but also inspiration and resilience. It took a lot of courage for these mothers to share their deepest pain. However, many have said that the act of doing so proved to be helpful on their journey. After digesting all of the contributions, I noticed the common beliefs these mothers held:

1. Grief is love. Grief is like the suitcase in my short story—full of love and cherished memories.

2. Healing requires the decision to move forward. It doesn't happen without work.

3. There will always be dark days. Eventually, the okay days will outnumber the dark ones and there will be

some good days, too. Survivors pick themselves up on the dark days, and treat themselves with compassion every day.

4. Each journey is different. What works for one person may not work for another. The important thing is to build a grief toolbox with several tools inside. If one tool doesn't work, you have others at your disposal. Keep adding new tools and use them often.

5. The path to HEALING is a thorny one. It has lots of cliffs, sharp rocks, and steep, exhausting trails. It is not an easy journey but each day you take a step, the climb becomes easier. In time, you may find that the rough mountain ahead of you has become a rolling hill with beauty tucked among the sharp rocks.

Journey to HEALING is about surviving the intense grief of child loss. My hope is that you will learn coping skills so you can live your new reality in a way that allows you to honour your child and live your best life. I will introduce you to new ways to heal your hurt and hope for a brighter tomorrow. *Journey to HEALING* will reveal seven basic areas of healing and actions. The personal experiences of bereaved mothers shared within this book will leave you feeling connected and hopeful so you can bravely carry on. It is my intention that *Journey to HEALING* will also become a valuable resource as you continue down the path through grief. As your needs change, you may find yourself being drawn back to certain parts of this book.

Each of the seven core chapters ends with a Check Point that asks you to pause and reflect on what strategies you can integrate into your HEALING journey now, and what barriers might be standing in your way.

As we travel down this road together my hope is that you will find courage and inspiration. I invite you to continue with an open heart and step onto the path that will take you on the journey to HEALING.

Hugs and much love to all of you,

XO Lisa

Contents

Part 3: The Map

Part 4: The Plan

Part 5: The Journey

PART 1

The Suitcase

CHAPTER 1

The Journey Begins

The doorbell rang just past 10 p.m. on a Tuesday night. Sitting in bed with books in hand, my husband and I looked at each other. Who on earth could that be? My husband made his way to the door. All I heard was, "Are you Darryl Boehm? Is your wife home?" I have never shot out of bed faster in my life. The man's voice was full of authority and I knew that something was horribly wrong.

Nothing could have prepared me for that moment or those words. It was the moment my life changed forever, when time became defined as before or after. Awful things happen all the time, but I never thought it would happen to my family or me. When a police officer and coroner visit your home, the news is never good.

It was like a scene out of a movie but there was no director and no script. "You folks better sit down," the officer said without haste as he sat on the ottoman across from us. How could I not know what he was about to say? He was so quick to deliver the news that

I didn't even have time to blink. "Your daughter Katie was involved in a fatal car accident. She died immediately."

I began to shake. Uncontrollably, like I never had before. The tears didn't come right away, but the shock set in instantly. Sitting on my couch with my husband at my side, eyes wide and unblinking, shaking in disbelief, my world stopped spinning.

I didn't really hear much after those life-altering words. I remember the officer being compassionate and kind but the specifics were quickly forgotten. One thing I do recall was the emphasis that Katie died on impact. The most unbelievable words came out of my mouth: "Thank God." I still question my sanity for thanking God for anything at that moment. Mind you, I think my sanity died that night, too.

Looking back at that moment, I am equally in awe and puzzled at how the human body and mind can shut down yet function at the same time. No feelings, no thinking—just disbelief and numbness. Survival mode. It's a good thing that breathing is an automatic physiological response because if I had to make the decision to breathe at that moment, I would not have been able to.

Devastated and numb, wide-eyed and stunned, and now burdened with the heaviest, darkest, and most devastating news of all, I pulled my husband and son closer. We had been handed the suitcase of grief, the bag of despair that we would carry forever.

My journey had begun...

~Lisa Boehm, mother of Katie, 17½ years old

Pregnancy was a magical time for me, and for many others too; our love growing each day with our baby. I can't think of any other time when we have so much love in our hearts for someone we have never met. But that is motherly love. It's unquestioning and it's powerful.

From the moment I knew I was pregnant, I planned for my babies to have a perfect life and all the advantages possible. I read all the parenting material I could get my hands on, took pre-natal classes, and talked to all my friends who were moms to find out more.

By the time each of my pregnancies was confirmed, my husband and I began creating hopes and dreams for our children. We were filled with excitement and joyous thoughts: *Maybe my child will make this world a better place to be. Maybe she will have her father's eyes or his grandfather's sense of humour.*

Becoming a mother changes us too. When we are carrying a child, we feed our bodies better, visit our doctors regularly, and pay close attention to our little wonder as they grow. The connection and love between mother and child starts in utero and in many cases we begin putting our child's needs ahead of our own. I think we all mature immensely when our children are conceived, no matter our age. We become selfless, nurturing, and more loving.

Let's be honest, becoming a mom is one of life's greatest honours.

Finally, after so much waiting and planning, we labour for hours with great anticipation to meet and hold our baby. I can't think of too many people that I would endure that pain for, but I'd do it ten times over for my children.

There is no love like the love between mother and child. No matter what they do or how they make us feel on occasion, we love them. Could anyone else rob us of sleep, push our buttons, and still be number one in our world? That's unconditional love. They test, they push, they challenge … yet we love them every day and every moment and thank our lucky stars as they sleep. We cheer them on in tough times, kiss their scrapes, and hold them tight. We think we know what love is until we have a child. Little did we know how much love our hearts can hold.

It's our job as mothers to keep our children safe and secure. During pregnancy, we ensure their safety by sleeping in certain positions, abstaining from alcohol and questionable foods, taking our prenatal vitamins, and keeping ourselves out of harm's way. Then once our little bundles are handed to us, we continue the job of keeping them safe. We secure them in government-approved car seats, take infant and child CPR, interview numerous daycares for the best option, put up safety gates, monitor their play, and introduce foods at exactly the right times as we watch for signs of allergy. It's exhausting, but we do it without even thinking. Our child is our world.

When you are handed the suitcase of grief, your journey through grief begins. Grief is ugly, burdensome, heavy, and exhausting to carry. The outside of the suitcase represents all the anger, bitterness, fear, guilt, blame, and regret that go with grief. The inside contains something altogether different.

The problem is you don't know where to turn or who to ask for directions. No one tells you what to do after your child dies.

It's as if you have been dropped into a foreign land and all you have is a horribly heavy suitcase in your hands. You have to drag it everywhere because it's so heavy. If you do pick it up and carry it, you stumble under its weight. It is so heavy you can't even think about anything else.

Everything is unfamiliar and the landscape is anything but welcoming. Where do you go? What do you do? You can't think straight and can barely walk, much less breathe.

Even when you are surrounded by people, you still feel alone. You are hopelessly lost and looking for answers, feeling helpless and abandoned. This foreign land is *grief.*

Those early days are all about survival. There's no sleep to be had and few calories pass our lips. Breathing is even a struggle. Our chests tighten and we feel like we might die. We hurt all over with a pain we have never known. During that time, family and friends keep us upright. They do their best to help us and wish with all their hearts they could take the pain away, even for an instant. They bring food, hold us, make phone calls, help with arrangements, and even ensure the Kleenex supply is kept up.

In some ways, the first few days are easier because we are kept so busy. We have visitors to receive, flowers to put in water, obituaries to write, and funerals to plan. Alone or with assistance, we choose our child's clothing for their burial or cremation, pick out their favourite music, and pour over photos for the service bulletin and slide show. Somehow we accomplish what we need to do. The days are filled with endless tears and total anguish, but surprisingly we push through.

Our child's name is continually spoken at the beginning of our journey and every interaction we have is because of them. We run on adrenaline for days, then fumes, then we crash when exhaustion sets in. For many of us, the hardest part of the journey begins when the funeral ends. All of our family, friends, and supporters go back to their worlds, which continue to spin while ours has stopped. The visits dwindle and feelings of isolation set in.

No matter our child's age or circumstance of death, the pain is intense and unrelenting. We mourn more than the loss of our child's life. We grieve a lost future that includes milestones such as graduation, convocation, promotions, marriage, and children of their own. There is also the loss of our future experiences and moments with our child. There will be no new pictures and no more Christmas or birthday celebrations. It is a loss so deep and so complex. There is nothing that compares to the death of a child.

Many believe that child loss is beyond the natural order of things. We should mourn the loss of our grandparents before our parents, and our parents before us. The thought of laying our child to rest never crosses our minds. Why would it? There are so many questions. Why do children have to die? Why mine? I'm willing to bet we have all had that conversation with the universe, God, or the powers that be, because it seems so wrong. It doesn't make sense and it's so incredibly unfair.

My daughter Katie was a 17-year-old senior at high school and had just received a $3,000 entrance scholarship to the faculty of nursing at our local university. She was the teenager that followed the rules. She was a good kid and one that would have done great things in her life. Katie was kind, hardworking, and had drive like I have never seen in a teenager. While I don't believe any life is more valuable than another, I can't help but wonder *why Katie?* Child loss is truly something no parent should ever have to endure.

The suitcase of grief had been handed to me like it has been handed to you and so many others. Now what would we do?

"Nobody said it would be easy, but nobody said it would be so hard either."

~*Patricia McIntyre, mother of Jason, 33 years old*

CHAPTER 2

Totally Unprepared

"I feel like I'm a walking contradiction. I feel strong, yet so weak. ... I feel like I have lived life to the fullest, yet I want to just sit and breathe ... I want to create memories and do things with my kids, yet feel so sad and broken doing things with them that Austyn should be here for. I feel so angry, yet so happy to have had Austyn and our family ... I feel frustrated with the lack of compassion and understanding. I think that's the best I've come up with is I'm a walking contradiction. And I am devastated that I have lived my happiest days—because I'll always have the "this would be better if Austyn was here" moments ... In some ways I love the part of me that seems to have been woken up by our tragedy, yet I hate her at the same time. It really changes day to day. I'm still in the fake it 'til you make it mindset but I am now able to fake it ... with a moment here and there of happiness."

~Rebeccah Schenstead, mother of Austyn, 19 years old

A study published by the National Center for Biotechnology Information says that child loss may be the greatest and longest lasting traumatic experience that someone can endure.[1] And I think anyone who has endured child loss would agree.

We are totally unprepared for the moment our child dies. We freeze in our tracks, fall to our knees, and try to catch our breath. Then we try to imagine how we will carry on. While the focus is our child who died, a part of us is lost forever too. Our role as a mother changes the moment our child dies.

The world we once knew has crashed down around us and life as we once knew it is forever changed. We prepared and studied for the arrival of our child, but there was nothing to prepare us for the anguish of loss. We sit amidst the fallen dreams trying to make sense of something that doesn't make sense.

At this point, we are fighting to survive—merely staying alive. It's the way our body and brain protect us, believe it or not. We shut out any unnecessary thoughts and tasks and instinct takes over. We sit in our grief and sleep since that's all the energy we seem to have. We continue to breathe, our hearts continue to beat, and our bodies continue to function.

Survival mode is not a desirable place to be. I sure didn't want to stay there. Yes, I was alive, but I felt like I had nothing left inside me and had no desire to continue on.

There were days that I wanted to die. Really wanted to die. The only thing that kept me from taking my own life was the voice of reason. It may have been Katie. She would have been so mad at me if I had followed through with that thought. So would a lot of people. I kept thinking about the devastation I would cause. How could my son possibly get his feet underneath him if I took my own life? And then I thought about my husband. How unfair would it be to leave him with a hurting teenager to raise on his own? I thought about it, believe me, but I never did anything about it.

This was all part of my reason to work on my healing. I could not and did not want to feel this way for the rest of my life, or even another week. I could not go on feeling so desperate and hopeless.

In 1969, psychiatrist Elizabeth Kubler-Ross authored a book called *On Death and Dying* after noticing a gap in the medical literature concerning grief. Specifically, she wrote about patients faced with terminal illnesses that faced their own mortality and the stages they went through until they ultimately accepted their mortality. Her theories also addressed the feelings of the patients' families and loved ones during this time. The Kubler-Ross model, also known as the five stages of grief, suggests that individuals move progressively through five phases of grief: denial, anger, bargaining, depression, and acceptance. According to this model, the stages follow one after the other, in a concise manner. Kubler-Ross later said that grief is not linear or predictable and felt that her work was misunderstood and regretted the confusion.[2]

The very first counsellor we saw after Katie's accident got an earful from me. How could a professional apply this model to us? I knew the model had been written about patients in the hospital who were in the stages of dying, not families like us who had been taken by surprise. I also knew early on that there was no separation of emotions—it was an intense mish-mash of feelings all at once. Our grief could not be categorized into neat little stages.

There is no doubt that we experience all of the emotions listed in this well-known model, but the truth is that the journey of grief after child loss is not a clear-cut path. Emotions cannot be compartmentalized and they are not experienced solely on their own. Researchers and professionals along the way have disputed the Kubler-Ross model for many reasons.[3] For starters, there are many more emotions than those outlined in the model, like blame, guilt, regret, and fear.

There is also the concept of progression that does not hold true. I have certainly experienced many emotions at once and go back and forth between them. After I experienced bargaining and depression, I moved back to anger several times and probably will continue to do so. It certainly hasn't been linear for me: it's more like a roller coaster of emotions, especially in the beginning.

The Kubler-Ross model also implies that after acceptance is reached (the last stage in her original model), the process is done. I accepted Katie's death early on, not that I liked it or was okay with it, but I acknowledged the fact that she had died and her life on earth was over. Am I done grieving? Absolutely not. Even today as I write this book in a lively coffee shop, I feel anger and sadness for what has been taken away from me.

The grief associated with child loss cannot be described or formulated by anyone who has not experienced it themselves. No disrespect to the numerous psychologists and professionals who have written books about grief and loss, but if you haven't walked this path you cannot know this path fully.

Child loss is in a category all its own. Please don't compare yourself and your journey to a textbook and theories. Your journey is *your* journey. We are all individuals and are unique in everything we do and our grieving will be just as unique.

Doing grief your way doesn't mean that you should stop trying to feel better or stay miserable for the rest of your life. It simply means that we shouldn't compare ourselves to a textbook or another person's journey. Your grief is as unique as your child.

I was at a real loss. The research I found had a lot of holes in it as far as I was concerned. I knew I wanted and needed to keep moving on this journey. I knew it wasn't a race and that no amount of hurrying would speed up the healing, but I refused to stay stuck. I saw others on this journey hold onto their grief with both hands and had no intention of letting go. They had no desire to begin healing. That scared me and I did not want to live like that.

With resolve, I started filling my days with anything and everything that made me feel a teensy bit better. I got out of bed every day, showered, and got dressed. I know not everyone can do that, but the longer I stayed in bed the worse I felt. I had to keep going.

Early on, I started setting the goal to do three things each day. Trust me when I say they were small things but it gave me a sense of purpose and accomplishment every day. Some days those three things included having a shower, loading the dishwasher, and throwing out the dead flowers.

When the house was quiet after my husband and son left in the morning, I would have coffee with Katie. When we first brought her ashes home, I set them on a table in the front room where the sun shines every morning. It seemed like a fitting place for her urn since a lot of wonderful memories were made in that room.

Each morning I'd pour myself a cup of coffee and sit with Katie's ashes, her picture, the growing pile of feathers I kept finding everywhere, and my memories. Call me crazy, but I believe she stopped by most days to say hi, too. I would sit for an hour or two and say things I needed to say to Katie or God. It really did make me feel better. Those chats were often filled with tears and me begging for direction. I was so lost.

Hearing myself ask for help over and over again made me realize that I wanted to heal. I hated feeling this way and really wanted to find some level of peace and a way that I could keep living without so much pain.

I tried everything. I read books, I met with other bereaved mothers most weeks, I tried counselling (and went through a number of therapists until I found one that was a good fit for me and my circumstances). I went to Reiki, had massages, and followed recorded meditations. I started following social media groups that offered guidance and tips for bereaved mothers. I was scrambling and reaching out in every direction possible.

I feel empowered when I am actively working on a project. I have always been that way, even before Katie's accident. Now I had the most challenging and important project in front of me: healing myself and supporting my son and husband as they healed, too. I knew the direction I wanted to move in but had to figure out how I would make it happen.

"Grief feels like a heavy coat I wear every day. But I feel gratitude for Liz—29½ years with her is far better than her never existing at all."

- Barb Tait, mother of Elizabeth, 29 years old

PART 2

The Direction

CHAPTER 3

Fork in the Road

"I have tried my best to leave Lane's accident in the past and focus on the future. A lot of people believe that the pain is the connection to their child who has died, but for me that wasn't where I wanted to be. I knew I had far more love for Lane than pain and I really focused on changing that grief into love.

I have learned that joy and pain can, and do, co-exist and you can build your love around your grief.

I think we make a choice every day about how we are going to be in the world. We make that choice over and over again each day. We can choose to be miserable and push people away from us, or we can choose to survive and to work on being okay every day.

Time does not heal all wounds. I believe it is what you do with that time that helps you learn how to coexist with the death of your children.

Deep down inside there is still the love you have for your child, a never changing love—a love that will always be there. Hold on. Keep breathing. The love is always there."

~Wanda Campbell, mother of Lane, 17 years old

My new reality: Katie was gone from this world and would not be coming back. I realized that this journey was not going to change. I was the only one who could travel this path. Even with my family by my side, I had to take my own steps towards healing.

I knew one thing for sure. I knew how I didn't want to grieve. I didn't want to be angry or bitter. I didn't want to be the person that people avoid talking to either. I needed people now more than ever. I wanted to be the kind of mom that could still give her son the brightest future possible. I knew the only way I wanted to be, and that was positive and grateful. Yes, I said grateful.

If I could undo the past, I would do it in a heartbeat, just like you would. There is nothing I wouldn't do to have Katie bust through the front door and tell me she was sorry for being late, that it was all a big misunderstanding. We've all learned there is no amount of bargaining or wishing that will change our reality. Our children are gone from this world, so now we must learn to navigate life without them.

I couldn't change what had happened, but I could choose the way that I travelled this road. If I was going to journey down this rocky path, I would have to be strong, I would have to be healthy, and I would have to have the right mindset.

During those early days and months, I imagined Katie watching me and wondered what she thought. I've only ever wanted to make her proud and smile from beyond. I dreamed of ways that I could honour Katie and keep her memory alive.

Then one day it hit me: if I was the one on the other side watching Katie and my family live their lives, I would want them to go on with their dreams, help people, laugh loud, and be happy. From that moment on, I chose to believe that is how she wants my family and me to be. She would be so disappointed if I gave up, isolated myself from the world, and lived in despair.

I choose to walk this road in a way that honours Katie and I want to walk it in a way that helps my son and husband cope with their grief. I want to be the mom that my son deserves and the mom that Katie would be proud of. My son was 15 years old when his sister died. I love him just as much as I love Katie, so it was an easy decision to live my best life for him too. The teen years are challenging enough for a young boy and now he had grief to deal with as well.

Ryan needed me and I vowed to support him every step of the way. I knew those early days were hard for him. He wasn't used to seeing us so utterly devastated and lost so he spent a lot of time with friends. That worried me. He was struggling and lost. I wanted Ryan home with us and I didn't want him to feel bombarded with extreme sadness when he walked in the door. I decided that I would carry my grief with grace—for him.

It was the easiest, yet hardest, decision on my journey. It was the easiest because given the choice; it was the only option for me. It was the hardest because now I had to figure out how I would make that happen.

Grief is the most unpredictable opponent I have ever faced. Grief is sneaky and grief is ugly. Grief does not play by the rules. You can ignore grief all you like, but it's still there, lurking in the shadows. You will have to learn to get along with grief. It will be with you for the rest of your life.

You might be at the fork in the road where I found myself too. Here, you have two choices. You can take the path that doesn't require much work at all. However, this path continually loops back to anger and pain. It doesn't get you very far. Those that choose this path can miss out on the love that goes with grief and the beauty that hides within the pain.

The other path at the fork in the road can be scary, and incredibly challenging. It has a lot of ups and downs and blind curves and is really hard to navigate. This is the path to healing. It is not an easy journey but it leads you to a place of peace. At first glance, I think most people will stay at the fork, scared and unsure. Maybe they will venture down the first path because the second path is too much to handle in the beginning. The challenging route is the healing path and it will be there when you are ready.

Life often has a way of presenting these forks in the road when we are facing challenges. There is a quote that resonates with me and I reflect on it often. "We can't always control what happens to us, but we can control how we react to it."

I know that I want to honour my daughter. I want to live in a way that makes her proud so I choose to live in a way that brings me peace. I want to help other mothers who are on this path. I don't want to let grief define me and I certainly don't want to be known as the person who let grief destroy her. If I leave any kind of legacy when I am gone, I hope that I am remembered as a woman who faced adversity, and did her very best to live with joy in one hand and grief in the other.

I see healing as the bridge between surviving and living, and refers to what we are actively doing to become healthy again. Healing doesn't have an endpoint and it certainly doesn't mean that the hurt will ever disappear. But it does involve finding peace and working towards feeling better. The thought that healing might actually be possible may cause you to shake your head and put this book down, but I assure you that it is possible.

There comes a time in our journey when reality hits. We are here on this earth in this life for as long as we are meant to be. We can choose to deal with our grief in a way that leads to some level of peace or let the pain and grief destroy us and all the good that still remains in our life. I don't know about you, but there is no way I can live in a black vortex of constant pain, darkness, and negativity.

There is one thing, and one thing only that stands in the way of healing. It's not other people, it's not the pain, and it's not the difficulty.

It's the *decision* to heal.

Change and improvement in your life cannot start until you decide to change. How you navigate your health, your grief journey, and ultimately who you are is up to you. I'm here to tell you that you have a say in your healing and you don't need to live in despair.

Healing is my choice and it is your choice too. I may not have control over the various traumatic events in my life, including Katie's accident. But what happened after that was, and still is, entirely up to me. Eventually we have to start putting one foot in front of the other. There is no other way and no other person that can truly help you until you decide to help yourself.

I made my choice to heal for a lot of reasons. The biggest reason is definitely to be a good mother and support for my son, but other reasons include feeling better and having better coping skills for the dark days that are a part of grief. If I wanted to help my family, I needed to make the decision to take care of myself mentally, physically, and spiritually. I chose the journey to HEALING.

In this book, HEALING stands for Honouring your child, Exercise and self-care, Assistance, Living your best life, Ideas and intentions, Nurturing your soul, and Gratitude. On my own journey, I have found these particular areas of coping the most helpful and in the following chapters I will outline each one in detail and suggest various ways to apply these strategies to your own HEALING.

When you choose HEALING, you are choosing to remember the good times; you are choosing to take care of yourself, and you are choosing to honour your child. I try to do the things that Katie never got to do and smile big like she did, dress up for fun events, and stay connected to who and what was important to her.

HEALING isn't about putting the past behind you. I will be the first one to say that I will never ever do that. But HEALING is a lot better than reeling in pain. If I want people to continue to ask me about Katie or share a memory of her, I can't be a disaster every time they do or they will stop.

Moving forward should never be confused with moving on. Moving forward means that you start to rebuild your life around your grief and the memories of your child. Moving forward is HEALING, and HEALING is love. It is discovering all the beauty that your suitcase of grief holds.

No matter where you are at, you can start on the path to HEALING.

"I still have days when I cry all the tears I have inside, but they are fewer, just small cracks to fill with love."

- Joan Colombier, mother of Clotaire, 18 years old

CHAPTER 4

Trust your Compass

"Right from the beginning, I knew that I had to choose the difficult path of living, healing, and eventually feeling joy again. My son had lost a sister. I could not let him lose his mother too, along with the capacity to see good in the world. I wanted so much for him to carry on and live an amazing life, so I needed to do the same. Alongside the tears and sadness, I showed him that we could laugh and still have enjoyable moments. The day after Geneveve died, I packed up our swimming towels, sunscreen, and snacks and met my best friend with her two boys for an afternoon at the pool. I knew that I needed to allow the light to enter into the cracks of our broken hearts.

My favourite mantra has always been, "I will feel joy again." I was determined that I would integrate this unthinkable event into my life story, that it would be part of my story. Although Geneveve's death changed every aspect of my life, I did not want it to be the only thing that defined my life going forward.

I knew that the task of healing and creating a new life would be, by far, the most difficult challenge I had yet to encounter in my life. When your child dies, pieces of you wither and even die and new parts grow. You are a different person and some of your friends will be able to relate to that new person and some won't.

I knew that the only thing I could do now was to be there for my son and to learn how to live without (my daughter) ... to learn to live with the darkness in one hand and the light in the other."

~Alyson Melenchuk, mother of Geneveve, 15 years old

I remember sitting in our home office trying to concentrate long enough to answer an email in some way that made sense. I glanced over at a form that I had printed out a few weeks prior. It was a form that I used for my health-coaching clients: a readiness-for-change questionnaire. I absently picked it up and glanced over it. I went through the list of questions on the paper and mentally answered each question as if I were being asked if I was ready to begin my healing journey. Then I realized I *was* ready for change.

I thought absently, *"Is it too early to begin healing?" Will people think that I am no longer mourning the loss of my daughter? Will they think I've moved on and I am over it?"* It's never too early or too late to begin healing—the perfect time to begin the journey is when you are ready. As for what others think? I've never had the energy to worry about it. My healing is about finding my footing in a way that works for me.

My desire to feel better mentally, physically, and spiritually outweighed my desire to stay in the misery. I could not take much more of the intense pain. I needed to be proactive in my health and my healing. No matter how well I feel or how much peace I have in my heart, I will always miss Katie and will never consider my grief complete.

I looked up at Katie's picture. She smiled down at me and I felt in that instant that I would do anything for her and anything for my son. I made the decision to move forward with the intention to heal and to learn to live with my grief. I knew I had to find a way to carry my grief every day for the rest of my life. But I wanted to find peace. I wanted to experience joy again. And I didn't want my family destroyed by Katie's death.

Not one to back down from a challenge, I felt that this was some kind of test and I would not fail. I had a daughter looking down and a son looking up to me for guidance on this uncertain path. I needed to help Ryan. He was watching to see how I would manage. If I fell apart, there was no way I would be any use to him. I was determined to help him and hold my little family together.

The symbol of a compass became very important to me. I even had one tattooed on the inside of my right wrist where I look at it several times a day. I would find my way and my family would be stronger than ever. We needed to trust our compass. I was ready for change.

Below is the Readiness for Change questionnaire that I am referring to. With permission, I have adapted it for healing after child loss. Answer the questions honestly. Perhaps you are ready to begin healing your broken heart and perhaps you are not. Either way is okay, but being aware of where you are at is helpful. Remember not to be hard on yourself. This is the most difficult and challenging journey you will ever take.

1. Have you ever felt like you might never heal? Y N

2. Are you willing to make HEALING
   a top priority? Y N

3. Are your tired of the overwhelming pain? Y N

4. Do you believe there are inherent risks if you
   do not choose HEALING?
   (i.e. relationships, health, etc.) Y N

5. Are you committed to working on your
   HEALING, even though it will
   prove challenging? Y N

6. Do you have support from friends and family? Y N

7. Besides health reasons, do you have
   other reasons for wanting to explore
   new ways to heal? Y N

8. Are you prepared to be patient with
   yourself when you encounter obstacles,
   barriers and/or setbacks? Y N

9. Do you believe that your child would want
   you to take steps towards feeling better and
   taking care of yourself? Y N

10. Do you believe that working on your
    HEALING will honour your child? Y N

*Adapted with permission from the American Council on Exercise *Readiness to Change Questionnaire.*

My guess is that you answered YES to five or more of the questions above. It is so hard to separate our feelings from logic. Your heart might be saying *I'm not strong enough, I can't think about healing.* Your head might be saying *I feel horrible and want to find ways to cope better.* Your head and heart might be fighting one another—both are valid and both are strong. Usually our heart is yelling louder than our head when we are in so much emotional pain.

You might be thinking *who cares if I feel better?* But if you can step outside yourself for just a minute, you might see that choosing to work on your healing truly is a good thing—for your physical, mental, spiritual, and emotional well being. And for your family. We cannot support others if we are not well. And if we are not well, we cannot find peace.

I realized early on that I could either help or hinder the healing of my husband and son. I choose to heal for them as much as I choose to heal for myself. Some days my journey had nothing to do with me, and everything to do with them. We are a family, a team, and there's nothing I wouldn't do for them.

Changing your thinking, your habits, behaviours, and mindset is challenging and complex. If you are ready to start feeling better and to start finding peace, then bring your suitcase of grief and join me on this path that we journey together.

Now that you have read a little bit about my story and my philosophy, I hope that I can offer you some tools to help you on this journey. Goodness knows there is not one simple and clear way through grief. Some days it seems like there is no path at all; only the vertical face of a mountain in front of us. My hope is that you will be able to find some useful suggestions to use on your personal journey.

Not every word or suggestion here may resonate with you, but I hope you are able to find something helpful in every chapter. All I ask, no matter where you are on your journey, is that you keep an open mind and an open heart.

"I know how to get up and take that first step. I know there is always a first step—the single one right before me."

-Christalee Froese, whose baby died at 10 weeks in utero, and author of Journey To Joy[4]

PART 3

The Map

CHAPTER 5

Healing vs. HEALING

"*When I began to consider how I healed following the trauma of Garrett's death, I wonder if I am actually healed. How do I know? It isn't as though healing is a destination and we all know we have arrived. Grief does not leave visible wounds and scars.*

There are days when I feel healed–days that I feel at peace with the knowledge that Garrett is alive in Heaven. Even though I miss him, I am content believing I will see him again, content to smile at the joy he brought to my life. There are days when I have the energy to reach out to other bereaved parents and offer comfort.

But there are days when a song on the radio will make me cry, or a stranger's innocent comment will make me angry. There are still days when I feel Garrett's death was unfair and not a circumstance I should be forced to own.

As the years have passed, the days of feeling healed have begun to outnumber the days of feeling hopeless. Trust that this will happen for you as well.

I have reached this place through many tears and a lot of support from others. I know that my healing was my responsibility—my choice. No matter how you choose to heal, recognize that your path to healing is your responsibility. Most importantly, you must keep moving forward along this path. If you are honest with yourself about what you need, and you allow others to help you meet those needs, you will be able to reach a place where you feel healed also."

~Melanie Delorme, *mother of Garrett, 8 years old, and author of* After the Flowers Die[5]

Both healing and HEALING are about finding your footing and learning to survive the heartache of loss. Healing doesn't have to be so painful. We can change the experience to a journey of love and find peace in our child's death. This has been the most meaningful journey of my life—painful and arduous, but definitely meaningful. It has been life changing.

The traditional way of healing makes us believe that we have to put on a brave face, push all the hurt deep down inside, and never talk about our child again. Sadly, this way of managing death does not serve anyone well and it's time we move toward a new way of grieving and healing.

Sometimes we avoid thinking about the love and beauty of our child's life because it hurts too much. As long as the pain overshadows everything else, we will never find peace. The old way of healing meant carrying our suitcase of grief and trying to hide it from anyone who may glance your way.

In the past, healing meant that there would be an end date to our grief. That there would be pain on pain on pain but then one day you would be *recovered*. Your anger, fatigue, and extreme sadness would just go away. You would be healed. People were told to keep busy and forget the past and move on. Just push down all your feelings and memories that make you cry and you'll be fine.

This old-fashioned approach doesn't encourage healthy healing. I can't imagine never speaking Katie's name again. She is and will always be a part of my life and someone I speak of often. This approach is counter-intuitive and extremely hurtful.

This is not the way I wanted to face my grief. I wanted to do it differently. I believe that healing is about integrating our grief into our life in a way that feels good to us.

Author and grief expert Tom Zuba says there is no such thing as closure and wonders why we keep talking about it. There is no moving on, only moving forward with the death of someone we love. This is the new approach in grief. After the death of his 18-month-old daughter, Tom grieved the old way; the way I've described above. In his book *Permission to Mourn*, he shares the old-style ways he tried to navigate her death and didn't know if he would survive. Eight years later, when his wife died at the age of 43, Tom knew he could carry on with the new tools he had acquired. If this wasn't enough for one human being to endure, Tom lost his 13-year-old son to a brain tumour five years after losing his wife.[6]

While I may not agree with all grief experts or approaches to living with child loss, I feel that Tom Zuba has found the way.

Tom says it best:

"Clinging to the belief that when someone dies, you, too, die forever–sentenced to spend the rest of your days in a living tomb in which there is no escape. The new way of doing grief is choosing to believe that even though the dream you held for your life may have died alongside your beloved–you did not die. In fact, like the caterpillar, you are in a cocoon of sorts–resting, growing, evolving, and expanding until it's time to emerge fully and fly."[7]

With adversity comes the potential for growth—if we choose that. It doesn't come right away. It comes with time and plenty of soul searching. I decided early on that I would make Katie proud and be a better person. I had been so absorbed in the minute details of day-to-day life that the important things didn't get the attention that they deserved. Sometimes it takes your world to be shaken to the core to see things differently.

Katie's accident and all the challenges I have faced have helped me realize that I can let grief swallow me whole and waste the life I have been given, or I can live in a way that honours my daughter's memory and make a difference in this world. I can take that grief and put it to good use. I can help grieving mothers on their journey, I can give scholarships in Katie's memory, and I can drive change for safer roadways. There's a lot that I can do with my grief. Grief will shape us all, but how it shapes you is your decision.

My life course changed direction completely the moment that Corporal Magee came to tell us that Katie wouldn't be coming home. I hate that Katie is dead. I hate that she is not here on her birthday, our birthdays, Mother's Day, Christmas, and every other day of the year. I hate it all, but I choose to believe that that horrific night shaped my life and made me a better person and mother.

The new way of HEALING means learning how to carry your suitcase of grief with grace and intention. It means show-ing off its glorious interior to the world. HEALING may go against all that you have learned about grief and it is certainly different from society's expectations of us. It's time to stop creating more pain for ourselves by ignoring our emotions and start walking the journey to HEALING.

Katie's death has brought huge meaning to my life. I have a different perspective on what I want my life to look like and how I want to be remembered. I choose to continue living Katie's legacy each day that I am here on this earth. Loss can convey a totally different meaning if we let it. You can find peace, connection, and re-direction. It can give *you* a second chance at life.

Yet … we continue to fight it. It's like changing our diet or trying to add exercise to our daily routine. You can't expect to be an expert on day one. It takes small changes and diligence to change our thoughts and efforts. It's hard work. We have to be open and willing to make changes in our thoughts and actions, but it is possible to live a life with more love and light than pain.

Now I want you to pause for a moment and think of one small thing that could be considered positive that has happened as a result of your child's passing. Don't let your heart get in the way: use your logic here. Has your family grown closer? Have you been able to pay it forward somehow in your child's memory? Are you more compassionate? Do you reach out to others more often? Did you help create change so that other children would be safer on the roads? Did you learn to slow down and enjoy the little things in life? Do you now say things to loved ones that you always wanted to?

You absolutely do not need to think for a second that your child's death was a good thing. That is not the purpose of this new thinking at all. It is simply an exercise in choosing to find some good in the way you move forward with their death. I appreciate the wake-up call Katie's accident gave me and how much closer my family is now because of my renewed focus on them.

Are you willing to try to make a change and think about things a little bit differently? This new approach to HEALING still encourages you to feel every single emotion. It's not about avoidance or pretending that life is all rainbows and roses. HEALING is about finding the strength to stand up on the hard days and having the desire to release the pain and find peace. It's about learning to live in a new way that feels right for you.

In order to follow this path, you must take care of yourself. It's not an option. You must also believe that you deserve to feel better. You cannot find love if you don't love yourself.

You will have to be willing to let go of the old beliefs regarding grief. Those beliefs are what hold us back and prevent us from finding the love and meaning in death. Your world has changed, that much is for certain. Open your heart and your mind and step onto the new road to HEALING. This is where you are meant to be.

The following chapters have been written in a way that will help you learn, reflect, and implement tools that can support you on your journey to HEALING. At the end of each chapter, you will find a Check Point that will ask you what tools you would like to implement as well as what Road Blocks (barriers) you perceive and what steps you can take. I strongly encourage you to stop at each Check Point and pencil in your thoughts. You will find a free download on my website where all the HEALING Check Points and Road Blocks are listed. This download is available here: https:// www.lisakboehm.com/your-healing-pathway.

Included in the upcoming section, are the tips and strategies that have helped me most. I hope they will assist you on your journey as well. Some of the suggestions may resonate with you and you may feel challenged by others. As you know, we are all different and as such are helped by different things. Please use the following chapters to find a path to HEALING that feels right for you.

"I hold on to the hope that there is more to this life. I have to. It is what keeps me sane."

~Janet Dvernichuk, mother of Josh, 21 years old

CHAPTER 6

ℋ — Honouring

"As a family, we tried to find some comfort in working with the Canadian Avalanche Foundation, raising money to help build a chalet for backcountry skiers and hikers, with all the latest equipment for providing weather bulletins, avalanche warnings and information about the current safety of the conditions. We told ourselves that we would do everything we could to prevent this kind of death from happening to other parents.

On July 12, 2003, the Kokanee Glacier Cabin was formally opened. It's a stunning three-story post-and-beam cabin set on the shores of Kaslo Lake, just north of Nelson in the West Kootenays of the Selkirk Mountains. The cabin sleeps 20 in summer and is a stepping-off point for hikers who want to explore this jewel of a park.

The cabin pays tribute to Michel and sixteen others who have died in avalanches in that area. The generators are never off at the cabin, and a light always shines, like a beacon. I take some comfort in that."

~*Margaret Trudeau, mother of Michel, 23 years old
and author of* Changing My Mind[8]

On this path to HEALING, honouring our children can be one of the easiest and most heartfelt things we can do. In fact, you may find that you are already doing this. Honouring is about remembering, paying tribute to, and sharing memories of our children. It helps keep their legacy and memory alive and helps us continue a relationship with them. It focuses on the love we have for our kids with the hope that their memory will live on through our acts of honouring.

On my own journey, this is one of my favourite things to do. I love to find different ways to honour Katie. That's partly how this book came to be. Honouring Katie is a pleasure and it feels good. I love to talk about my girl and am always finding new ways to keep her memory alive. There are many things I have done to honour my daughter over the years, but one that particularly feels good is reaching out to other mothers who struggle with loss. It fills my heart and helps me feel happy. Honouring comes naturally to a lot of people, so it's a great place to start.

When I first started carrying my suitcase of grief, the darkness and heaviness of the despair was more than I could handle. It was easier to lay on the floor with my suitcase smothering me than it was to think about anything else. But once I made the decision to get up and live with my grief, I was able to open that big, ugly bag and see all the beauty inside. That beauty was all the love and meaning that Katie's life was and will always be to me. Once I was brave enough to focus on the incredible light inside my grief, the more I was able to focus on living, HEALING, and learning to carry my suitcase of grief.

Honouring is as diverse as our children. It can range from painting a picture to creating memory quilts, establishing scholarship funds, random acts of kindness, and a hundred other ways. Honouring can be public or private. The whole idea is to express your love as you learn to live with your grief and find peace. Your only limitation is your creativity.

One of the first ways we honoured Katie after she died was plan her funeral. As heartbreaking as it was, we wanted it to be perfect for our girl. We deliberated over the music and photos for the slide show; poured over the songs, poems, and stories, and searched for the ideal venue. We wanted to ensure that everyone left Katie's service feeling like they knew her a little bit better and how much she was loved. Every decision regarding our child's funeral is an act of honouring.

It's healthy to pour your energy and efforts into honouring your child. It helps bring some peace and a tiny sense of control when we are feeling so helpless. I remember looking at Katie's department store-sized closet and feeling overwhelmed. At first I thought I would box up her beautiful clothes and give them to a charity that helps women get back on their feet and into the workforce, but when a friend suggested a closet party I knew that is what I would do.

A closet party, you ask? I invited Katie's friends to look through her closet and take any clothing that reminded them of her. At first, the girls were quiet as they poured over the clothes I had spread out in three rooms. My house looked like a mini version of Macy's that night, but I am sure Katie was with us and loving every minute. As the evening wore on, the giggles got louder and the stories began to come out. One young lady claimed a sweater that she remembered buying with Katie and told us a hilarious story about the purchase. It was a lovely evening with Katie's friends sharing amusing stories and all of us having a few laughs. It felt right and it brought a wee bit of HEALING to everyone.

Over the last couple of years, I have come to an important conclusion: the only way that Katie's memory will be kept alive is by doing things in her memory and saying her name every day. I will continue reminiscing and telling stories and doing the things she loved. I find that the more things I do in her memory, the more content I feel.

Finding ways to honour Katie has brought a great deal of peace and love into my life. Taking action and working on my HEALING helps me carry my grief suitcase. Grief experts agree that honouring and remembering our loved ones is essential for healing. When bereaved parents continually do things in memory of their kids, experts like J. William Worden believe those parents are better equipped to live with their grief. He says we need an ongoing emotional connection with our loved one which allows us to keep living.[9]

Dr. Worden, a psychologist, developed a bereavement-recovery theory about living with grief. His theory is called *the tasks of mourning.* This philosophy not only includes remembering our children as a necessary step in our mourning, but also highlights the need for families and friends to remember and honour them in a way that is meaningful. Dr. Worden says that loss of a loved one makes us feel like we've lost control, but honouring and remembrance give us a sense of power. No matter how we do it, it's the action of honouring that is the important part.[10]

Honouring our children is a way of carrying our child with us in our new reality. They are still a part of our lives and honouring them provides one way that grief can co-exist with joy and happiness.

There is no right or wrong way to honour your child and there is no perfect time. I like to work on projects when the house is empty and I am alone with my thoughts. I do small projects somewhat regularly, like making photo books every few months, and do bigger projects when the time seems right. For example, Katie was in Grade 12 at the time of her car accident. When her would-be graduation date got closer, I discovered that some girls and their families struggle to find the money to purchase a fancy dress for graduation. Now, each spring, I collect gently used grad and bridesmaid dresses to donate to her high school. It makes my heart feel full and is a wonderful way to honour Katie. Goodness knows she loved dressing up and would be proud to be a part of such a meaningful project.

Listed below are some ways that you can honour your child. This list can be expanded to include many other activities. The only limit is your imagination. I encourage you to pick two or more things that you would like to do to honour your child in the coming days and weeks.

- Host a closet party (allow your child's friends to pick out a few pieces of clothing).
- Wear your child's favourite colour.

- Listen to their playlist or make one that reminds you of them.

- Watch their favourite movies (Katie loved *Home Alone* and all Christmas movies).

- Hold parties for their birthdays, angel-anniversaries, and other special days.

- Purchase a bench with a dedication plaque to be placed in a special location.

- Release balloons (not the greatest choice for the environment).

- Release butterflies (I used a Canadian company called Butterfly Wings and Wishes www.butterflyab.ca).

- Release ladybugs.

- Host a *Light up the Night* for your child (everyone brings a solar light).

- Create scholarships or awards in your child's name (talk to your local high school's guidance department).

- Help out a cause that is meaningful to you or your child.

- Help out the people that mattered to your child (i.e. their friends).

- Act in a certain way they would have wanted.

- Write a book, poetry, or journal dedicated to your child.

- Make or ask a trusted person to make quilts, blankets, or pillows out of your child's clothing.

- Have memorials made by glass blowers like Artful Ashes.

- Have jewellery made from your child's ashes or fingerprint (such as Solitude and Soul in Regina, SK, CA).

- Create photo books (Mixbook is so easy to use).

- Create artwork, picture collages, and jewellery (YouTube has lots of videos to get you started on any project).

- Decorate a space that is a special place to be with your child (i.e. their bedroom).

- Create a blog for sharing feelings and memories about your journey.

- Create new traditions in their memory (i.e. decorating the Christmas tree with white angels, etc).

- Create prayer flags.

- Plant a special garden dedicated to your child (in your own yard, local park, or your child's schoolyard).

- Talk about your child and tell "remember when" stories.

- Give some of their special belongings to others who may use them in your child's memory (i.e. dance/ sports gear).

- Volunteer with their favourite charity (i.e. humane society).

- Be a better person just because.

- Take care of yourself.

- Participate in an activity you shared with your child.

- Cook your child's favourite meals.

- Get tattoos.

- Renovate the backyard or place they liked to spend time.

- Erect a cross along a roadway.

- Wear their clothes, jewellery, hats, etc.

- Take a special holiday to a place that was so much fun for your child or travel somewhere they always wanted to go.

- Leave their ashes somewhere special, like the ocean or a place they loved.

- Paint meaningful objects or canvases. (One mom painted her son's motorcycle helmet).

Check Point
It's time to check in with your healing.
What are two new ways you can honour your child?

_____

_____

_____

Road Block
What is standing in your way?

_____

_____

_____

What can you do to remove this barrier?

_____

_____

_____

Keep Going
What are the next steps to making this happen?

_____

_____

_____

What steps can you take this week?

_____

_____

_____

"As a parent you always want what is best for your children. As a bereaved parent you want to ensure your child is always remembered; that you honour their precious memory. I think of Hannah and Nolan and carry them in my heart every day. Some days it is easier than others to find peace and put one foot in front of the other."

~Janet Patterson, mother of Hannah and Nolan, 1 day old

CHAPTER 7

E – Exercise and Self-care

"... Love yourself enough to know that as a woman, and especially as a mother, you have to take care of yourself first, before you can take care of others. We can get swept up in tornadoes of activity, trying to conquer the storms in our lives. Instead, I've had to learn for myself that I need to go to the eye of the storm, the quiet centre, to be able to see clearly and get perspective on why everything is spinning out of control around me. This usually means really taking the time to try to still your mind and listen to your intuition. For most women I know, as it was for me, this seems like a selfish approach to life. We can get caught in the trap of feeling guilty about not putting the needs of our children, our husbands, or even our employees or boss before our own. It's not true that it's "selfish." It's called "self-love"... Children need a healthy mother to create a

healthy home. The airplane-emergency metaphor holds a deep truth: "First put on your oxygen mask and then assist your child." I once asked an airline attendant why this was the direction. She told me that if the airplane ever lost altitude quickly, it would only take seven to fifteen seconds to lose consciousness. Obviously if you have blacked out, your ability to help your kids is zero."

~*Marie Osmond, mother of Michael, 18 years old and author of* The Key is Love.[11]

When you are in survival mode, exercise and self-care may seem like the last thing you care about but it has a huge impact on the way you feel. Studies have shown that exercise can be more effective than an antidepressant and proper nutrition can help with sleep, anxiety, and depression.[12] And sleep … we all know that good sleep makes everything better.

You might be rolling your eyes right now and are probably thinking, "Yeah, I know I should eat better but I just don't care about that right now. And exercise?! Is she kidding? And sleep?? Ha!" Bear with me and I will explain.

Exercise, nutrition, sleep, and water intake are critical and the basic building blocks of HEALING. The mind-body-spirit connection is undeniable. When we fuel one and strengthen it even a little bit, it helps the other aspects too.[13]

The best comparison I can think of is your car. You would never dream of taking your car on a demanding mountain journey without making sure it's in tip-top shape. You'd make sure it was fuelled up with the best gas, not cheap stuff that will cause the motor to burn out before you get to your destination. You would consider which tires were going to have the best grip for the steep and rocky paths and ensure the brakes were in excellent condition. You would also check the oil and other fluids.

Your body is not much different. If your food is lacking in quantity or quality, you simply will not have the energy to heal or even feel like you can survive. If you are physically incapable of holding yourself up, you won't be able to cope on this journey. We need to be as healthy as possible to travel this road.

Sleep is the fuel that can be extremely hard to come by, but is critically important for your mental well being and your physical health. We all know how lousy we feel after a crummy night's sleep. After child loss, one night becomes a multitude of crummy nights, which leads to utter and complete exhaustion. I haven't met many mothers who are getting the much-needed rest they need. Many of us close our exhausted eyes only to be confronted with insomnia.

Add in the recommendation to increase our water intake and it all becomes overwhelming.

There is so much information in the areas of exercise, nutrition, hydration, and sleep that they each deserve their own chapter or book for that matter. The science is overwhelming and the options for easy implementation in these areas are plentiful. On my own journey, while I have tried everything in an effort to feel better, I truly believe that these components are what gave me the tiny boost to believe that I might be able to survive my daughter's death.

Exercise is simply moving your body in a way that feels good. I had been an active person before Katie died and I needed to keep moving. Even though we lost Katie in December, winter was very mild that year, so I was able to get outside often. I could walk and let my mind wander. I wore my sunglasses even on the cloudiest days and cried. I walked for miles that first year. I'd walk so far sometimes, I thought I'd never get home, but I did. There is something about fresh air and the escape to the outdoors that can be so incredibly HEALING.

It doesn't matter *how* you move, but your body will definitely appreciate the love you show it. You've heard about endorphins before—the feel-good hormones that come after physical exercise, like a runner's high. Endorphins were my drug of choice after Katie's accident. They were addictive and I did what I could to get that high as often as possible. Even if I tossed and turned all night and had a total of three minutes sleep, I knew that moving my body would make me feel better. It wasn't pretty. I had bags upon bags under my eyes and felt completely beat up, but I'd crawl down to my treadmill or head outside. I would never call myself a runner. I'm more of a plodder, but I ran that first winter. I ran until I could barely walk back up the stairs because my knees hurt so badly. You're probably thinking, "Why would she do that? Why would she cause herself more pain?" The answer: endorphins. If I could get a five-minute, feel-better surge of endorphins that made me feel like I could survive another day without Katie, then I did it. I got a little bonus too—sleep came much easier when I exercised.

The combination of fresh air during the walks and the sheer exhaustion from the plodding runs on the treadmill knocked me out, even for a short while. The little naps or extended night sleeps gave me a teeny bit more hope that I might eventually be okay. Do you see how this all works together? Don't worry. I'm going to lay out some really easy ways to help you get moving, too.

Take a moment to reflect. What have you done in the past for exercise that you enjoyed? Did you go to yoga with a friend? Enjoy aquacize? Or, perhaps there was an activity that your child enjoyed that you would like to try? My sweet girl was a dancer and in the off-season she would ride her bike to a big hill about ten kilometers away, run up and down the hill as many times as she could, then bike home. Occasionally when I am feeling energetic, I try to do this and smile afterwards. Exercise doesn't have to be extreme, though. It's really about moving your body in a way that makes you feel good and brings HEALING to your body, mind, and spirit.

Nutrition doesn't have to be crazy and extreme either. Nutrition is about putting better fuel in your body and it doesn't have to be perfect. All of the recommendations in this book are meant to be easy and achievable. Getting back to the car example, you wouldn't put Kool-Aid in your gas tank and expect your car to function. Your body is not much different.

I remember for about a week after Katie's funeral, we lived on whatever was in the fridge; most of it was food from kind-hearted friends and family. When that ran out, I cringed at the thought of going anywhere in public so we ate out of the freezer for about another week. I used up everything and anything that was edible in the house and made some pretty weird meals.

After those supplies were exhausted I knew I had to go to the store but was too tired to think about my usual meal planning. I stuck to the basics. And you know what? It worked out okay. I bought fruit and vegetables, fresh chicken, pork, fish and beef, and stocked up the rice and quinoa supplies. For ages, we ate a protein, a carbohydrate, and a vegetable for supper because it was easy and I didn't really have to think about it. Having said that, there were many days in the beginning that I couldn't multi-task and we ended up with a big plate of chicken and nothing else. I hope I'm not the only one.

My point is that with all the choices in the grocery store and all the advertising on TV, it can really get overwhelming to think about healthy eating. You certainly don't need a formal plan, either. Just make better choices. Reduce the drive-through visits, drink more water, and focus on adding more nutrient-dense foods to your diet, like fruits and vegetables.

Do you want to know the easiest "meal" to make that can be super healthy? A smoothie. Not a sugary milkshake but a delicious mix of healthy ingredients. I remember thinking if I had one healthy meal every day, I was doing okay.

Here's an example of one of my go-to recipes:

Morning Green Smoothie:

- ½ cup pasteurized, liquid egg whites (egg whites in a carton). Yes, this is safe as long as they are pasteurized.
- ½ cup almond milk
- 1 TBSP sunflower seeds
- 1 TBSP sesame seeds
- 1 handful of raw spinach
- 1 frozen banana (the spotty kind for natural sweetness)
- 1 TBSP Matcha Tea powder (found at any health food store)
- 1 tsp. vanilla extract
- ½ TBSP minced ginger

Some of these ingredients might be foreign to you, but they are calming, easy to digest, give a gradual boost in energy (I love Matcha for that reason), and can help you start your day off on the right foot. It's my gift of self-care every morning.

Another easy go-to meal that I still eat most days is scrambled eggs with sautéed veggies. I usually sauté spinach, tomatoes, mushrooms, and zucchini then mix in two eggs and serve with either fruit (I love fruit trays for the ease) or toast and jam. Easy peasy and includes everything I need.

There is a lot you can do for yourself simply by making better choices. Focus on adding in healthy stuff instead of having the mindset that you should avoid certain things. The more you add in the good food, the less room you will have for the not-so-good stuff.

There can be a lot of memories associated with certain foods. Enjoy those memories and the food. Katie loved Dirt Cake, sweets, and everything loaded with sugar. She was incredibly health-minded for a teenager, but when given the chance, she gave in to her sweet tooth. If we are celebrating or hosting friends, I want to live and that means a little indulgence. Indulgences are all right, but try to stick to the healthy stuff as much as possible.

We think that sugar and caffeine help us feel better, but they can actually make us feel worse. So I try my best to make sugar an occasional thing and be mindful of my caffeine intake. The science tells us that sugar-containing foods and drinks inhibit serotonin and can lead to depression and irritability.[14] Ingesting sugar starts off making you feel pretty good. But we all know it's temporary and in the end we are left with the low.

Water seems like such an insignificant thing but even mild dehydration can trigger depression and can also cause insomnia leading to increased anxiety.

Processed foods (any packaged food with a barcode) can increase depression, too. In fact, there is a 58% increase in the rate of depression in those who eat a diet comprised of packaged and processed foods versus those who eat whole foods (foods grown and raised in nature).[15]

Foods that have a calming effect include turkey, chicken, milk, oats, cheese, nuts, and peanut butter. These foods all contain tryptophan that is a precursor to serotonin—the happy hormone. How about a turkey and cheese sandwich on grainy bread with a side salad or fruit? That's easy enough.

Now let's talk about vitamin B. Low levels of Vitamin B can intensify or trigger depression. Long before I lost Katie, I battled depression and anxiety and found that taking a vitamin B supplement made a huge difference. This helpful vitamin is also found naturally in foods such as beef, pork, chicken, leafy greens, oranges, rice, nuts, and eggs.[16]

Here is a quick reference to help you make better choices on this journey.

Eat More of this:	**Eat Less of this:**
___Water	___Sugar
___Fresh fruit	___Alcohol
___Fresh veggies	___Processed foods/chips
___Salmon, tuna	___Fast foods
___Greek yogurt	___Coffee/tea/caffeine
___Meat/high protein foods	___Soda/pop/sugary drinks
___Eggs	___Fruit juice
___Cheese	___Chocolate milk
___Nuts	___Breakfast cereal
___Beans/lentils	___Cereal bars/ready to go food

Sweet, underappreciated sleep—it's the one thing that we don't even think about until we don't get it. Looking back, I don't think I averaged more than about five hours a night for the first year after Katie died, and that was with the help of a sleeping pill. I managed okay without an antidepressant, but without sleep I was a disaster. My emotions ran particularly raw without sleep. And boy, oh boy, did I get mad. I became an out-of-control crazy person, which didn't really help anyone or anything.

Our life-changing news was delivered at approximately 10 o'clock at night, so for a long time I had a fear of going to sleep. If my son Ryan wasn't home, I was frightened that the police and coroner would come to the door again with bad news about him. I could distract myself all day and be somewhat okay, but as soon as I climbed into bed my mind would start racing. All the sadness and worry would sit heavy on my chest every night. Needless to say, falling asleep was a challenge for me for a long time.

I take sleeping pills and do a lot of self-care. After three years, I can sleep a solid, restful 7.5 hours most nights. I eat well, avoid caffeine after noon, exercise four-to-five times per week, and go for evening walks. I meditate, catch up with 20-minute naps if necessary, go to hot yoga in the winter, and see a therapist to unload and help me think more rationally. HEALING really is work.

I was fortunate enough to be able to be off of work for ten months, therefore I was able to dedicate a fair bit of time to self-care. I realize not everyone has that luxury. If you are in a position that you have to return to work sooner rather than later, perhaps you can ask for reduced hours to help you ease into work and allow yourself a wee bit more time to take care of yourself.

Early on, my doctor talked to me about sleep hygiene. At first I felt like a two-year-old getting advice about sleep, but it really did help. Sleep hygiene refers to our bedtime routines. If we let our emotions run our circadian clocks, our sleep issues may get worse before they get better. Instead, choose your bedtime and stick to it as much as possible. For me, that's 10 p.m. I start to wind down at 9:30, close down all electronics, including TV, take my sleeping pill, and then do something relaxing. On a cold night, I will have a warm bath and read a book and some nights I listen to a guided sleep meditation. But every single night, I climb into bed between 9:45 and 10 and read a fluffy, mindless book.

Sleep is probably my biggest struggle if I am perfectly honest, but I feel it is improving. My naturopathic doctor has recommended supplements for a variety of issues including sleep, but I find that my own habits play just as big a role as the supplements. If I get too anxious about something, no amount of supplements or reading will work. Sleep is a constant project for me.

Water. Our bodies are 65% water and we lose small amounts of it all the time due to urination, sweating, breathing (the moisture in our breath, specifically), and crying. The more caffeine we consume, the more dehydrated we become, too. The same is true for alcohol. There is nothing better than water. Think of all the tears you have released. You have probably cried litres and litres of tears. That must be replenished or you will feel even worse than you already do.

Dehydration can cause headaches, increase brain fog, and make you more tired.[17] We feel rotten enough as it is. We don't need to feel any worse.

Fill a water bottle and carry it with you everywhere. Take sips when you think about it. Drink a full glass of water after you eat, or every time you walk by the kitchen sink. Ask someone to bring some bottled water to keep in your fridge.

Aim for eight cups per day. Juice, milk and other beverages don't really count as water, but they are better than caffeinated beverages or alcohol. Do your best to make all your beverages water.

Here are ways to integrate exercise into your day:

- Walk. Get outside if at all possible, check out a local indoor track, or use a treadmill. This can be a great time to connect with friends if you are feeling up to it. Aim for 20 minutes or more.

- Exercise DVDs/live streaming (i.e. Beachbody)

- Sign up for an exercise class/yoga/Pilates

- Run

- Bike or cycle indoors

- Contact a personal trainer

- Rent a stand-up paddle board or kayak or canoe

These are some ways to help improve your sleep quality and duration:

- Go to bed at the same time every night

- Turn off electronics 30 minutes before bedtime

- Avoid all caffeine after noon

- Read a book instead of watching TV after 9 p.m.

- Drink a warm cup of decaffeinated tea instead of snacking in the evening to help your body wind down

- Get some physical exercise in the day

Here are some strategies to help you drink more water:

- Drink a glass of water after waking up in the morning

- Drink a glass of water with each meal

- Find a 1-litre (4-cup) water bottle and aim to drink two of these bottles per day

- Keep the fridge stocked with bottled water

***Tip—making your smoothies with water counts toward your daily water intake as well.

Check Point
It's time to check in with your healing.
What are two new ways you can improve your physical well being?

_____

_____

_____

Road Block
What is standing in your way?

_____

_____

_____

What can you do to remove this barrier?

_____

_____

_____

<u>Keep Going</u>
What are the next steps to making this happen?

_____

_____

_____

What steps can you take this week?

_____

_____

_____

"I take care of my body, mind, and soul and the more I do, the more whole I feel and better able to deal with life. I can do things. I just take Michael along in my heart."

~Ariella Long, mother of Michael, 20 years old[18]

CHAPTER 8

A — Assistance

"When really, really bad things happen, we have to be intentional to reach for what is positive and what is good.

One thing I've learned along the road of my own grief journey is that you develop strategies and tools that help you cope. They say time heals all wounds; I'm here to tell you that simply is not true, at least not when it involves the loss of a child. Time, along with the support and help of friends, family and even strangers, does make the intensity of the waves of emotion a little less each day and the waves are a little farther apart.

Those moments, as I've found, are a double-edged sword. On one hand they crush me, but on the other hand, they remind me of how much I loved my son. I have a saying now that is simply, "We grieve as deeply as we loved." So, when I experience those moments I remind myself that my son was loved, by me and by many others ... and those times bring a sense of warmth and comfort to me. I embrace those moments instead of fighting them.

There will be denial, anger, blame … there will be an over-whelming scope of emotions that will go from one extreme to another. If there is one piece of advice I can give, or at least an insight on what helped me … let people help! People care, people love you and people simply won't have words that will help but know that they are there to support you.

Know that you can get through this. It's a journey that will never end for you and your families but a journey you don't travel alone."

~Jan and Barry Stewart, parents of Ken, 29 years old

Learning how to carry your suitcase of grief is not an easy task, which is why it's so important to reach out for help. Assistance can be found with support groups, grief counsellors, others who have suffered loss, the church, medical doctors and naturopaths, as well as friends and family: anyone who is able to help you. While I encourage you to find the people or groups that are the best fit for you, I also recommend that you utilize as many supports as you can. There is no shame in asking for help.

Assistance can be many things—it can be cleaning the house, buying groceries, or helping with the children. It can be sharing, talking, and leaning on one another. It can be counselling with a professional or it can be getting help with mood-stabilizing medications. It might be a holistic approach with an entire team.

People will inevitably say, "If there's anything I can do, please let me know." Usually we are in too much of a fog to have an answer to that question, even though we need help.

Having our driveway shovelled that first winter by neighbours was such a relief. A friend dropped by with non-perishables, toilet paper, and Kleenex so we didn't have to venture out of the house for another few days. All of these gestures were very thoughtful and so appreciated. The day before Katie's service I asked a neighbour if she could buy some champagne and a few champagne glasses. It took so much stress away from me. Little things like that may seem insignificant to those helping, but when you are deep in grief, those little things are big things and so meaningful.

The fact of the matter is most people will offer to help, and wait for your direction. Everyone is hurting for you, but they don't know how to help. Ask them. Text or email if it's easier. Ask them to pick something up from the store or make a batch of muffins. This will help them help you. When someone calls and asks, "Do you need anything?" feel free to say, "Yes, I could use a few bananas and a loaf of bread" or whatever it is that would make things a little easier for you. And don't be afraid to ask for a healthy meal. If one of your friends is a keener in the kitchen ask her to prepare you something. She will be happy you asked.

I strongly feel you should involve your doctor in your care. Most bereaved mothers that I know have needed the assistance of antidepressants, at least temporarily, and many have needed sleeping pills. There is no gold medal for getting through this without medication. If you are currently managing without, it's important to continue with regular doctor visits in case your needs change. I have only needed sleeping pills and I strongly believe that is because of the healthy lifestyle and coping mechanisms that I have incorporated over the years. However, I am not adverse to the idea of prescription medications if my coping abilities change. They are there for a reason, so please consult your physician. Together you will figure out what's best.

Be aware that patience is required when starting antidepressants. Unfortunately, they do not work overnight. In fact, most take upwards of six weeks to kick in. This is also why counselling is highly recommended—to bridge the gap and get support while waiting for the medication to start working.

I would also like to say a few words about naturopaths. They take a very holistic look at your life and can make suggestions for your diet and supplements that may prove beneficial. Be prepared to answer a lot of questions since naturopaths look at everything going on in your life. There may be dietary recommendations as well so be ready for that.

My experience on this journey has led me to create a support team. I have sought help from everyone you can imagine. Some have stayed on my team the entire time and some only for a short while. I sought a Reiki practitioner in the early days that helped me let go of my fears of losing my son and how to put his struggles in perspective. Later, I found help from a wonderful naturopath who helped me with a myriad of problems, both physical and emotional. Find practitioners that are a good fit for you. Keep an open mind and don't be afraid to reach out.

These resources do cost money and that may be a stretch for you. If you have a benefits package at work, inquire about how these services might be covered. Some companies also have private counselling services that can be accessed at no cost. If these resources do not exist for you, check for free resources online. Here in Regina where I live, there is free online counselling through the university and you are not required to be a student to access the program. The government and provincial health authority support this important resource. What a wonderful option for anyone struggling with mental health.

My husband, son, and I went to a group counselling session a couple of times. I thought this was going to be the perfect fit for us. However, the young counsellor really didn't seem to have a clue and we all left frustrated.

In fact, it was a disaster.

The key with counselling is to be patient and find a professional that feels right.

For us, it wasn't group therapy. My husband and son found their own ways and I found a counsellor that worked for me. It took me a while to find the right person, but I have found a psychologist who *gets* me and understands loss. I think that you must find someone with whom you can really connect and feel comfortable with.

I feel like I'm in a place now where I may not need regular visits with my counsellor but I still schedule appointments. Inevitably, there is something I need to talk about when I go. And if I'm heading into a tough time of the year, like Katie's birthday or her angel anniversary, I book extra appointments. It's one thing to talk to family or friends about your journey, but a professional is best equipped to help you, not just listen. If you are not sure who you should see, ask your doctor or ask other bereaved mothers you know if they can recommend someone. Then pick up the phone and make an appointment. Don't wait.

Support groups can be incredibly helpful on this journey and I consider them to be an important part of my HEALING.

When it comes to support groups, try to find one that aligns with your beliefs and needs. Perhaps you would like the support of a religious-based group, or maybe you would prefer being in the company of mothers who meet regularly for coffee, crafts, and sharing. I need to be surrounded with women who *get it*, who have the desire to work on their HEALING, and choose a positive outlook as they learn to live again.

As you know by now, the grief that accompanies child loss is unlike any other kind of grief, so make sure you find a circle that speaks directly to child loss and offers the comfort you are seeking. Online groups can be very helpful too, especially when you feel like you are not ready to face people yet.

I was extremely fortunate. I was invited into a child loss support group right away. We lost Katie in early December and the mothers in this group were having a get-together right before Christmas. I remember putting the date on my calendar thinking I'd never go to something like *that*. The thought of a support group for bereaved mothers made me think of a swirling black vortex of sadness that I did not want to be a part of. Yet, as the day grew closer, I thought I would go and check it out. Even if I didn't cross the threshold, I challenged myself to go. Oddly enough, I had to drive the stretch of road where Katie died to get there. It was getting foggy and I drove it with white knuckles, but I did it.

When I arrived, I was greeted with the biggest, warmest hug I have ever received. I hadn't met this kind woman before, yet it seemed like I had known her all my life. I felt like this was exactly where I needed to be. I stayed for four hours.

Support groups come in many shapes, sizes and approaches, so I suggest you look around. They are not one size fits all. You need to find one that works for you, where you leave feeling better than when you got there. If you leave feeling frustrated or angry or worse than when you arrived, you are not in the right place.

People can be difficult. You may find that some friends and family are able to support you in one area where others may be supportive in a different area. While it can be frustrating to discover that some people disappear into the woodwork, it is astonishing how some people can be so supportive at a very trying time. I feel like the number of friends in my life since Katie died is still the same as before, but some have gone and some have stayed and some are new.

There will always be well-intentioned people out there who will try to connect with you and try to support you. However, they try to show empathy by sharing stories of a favourite grandparent who passed away or God forbid, their dog that died. Try to take a breath and remember that they are only trying to make you feel like you are not alone, as frustrating as their words may be. I have to remind myself that all loss hurts and this is their frame of reference to our loss.

Sadly, not everyone is going to be equipped to help you, either. This was a big lesson for me. The people you assume will be in your corner may not be able to support you now. It's terribly frustrating but it's true. I wasted many hours and lots of energy stewing over this, but it is simply out of our control. You will gravitate towards those who are capable.

I am still amazed at the number of people who have stepped into my life because they knew I needed support. It's like they were sent from heaven knowing I would be on this journey. Whatever the reason, I am eternally grateful for those who have stayed close. I know it's been hard to be strong when I am weak or find the right words, but it is so appreciated.

It's really important to find support and your personality will likely dictate your preferences. Do you prefer to speak to one person in a quiet setting? Some people feel overwhelmed

in a group setting while others may feel comfort in this scenario. You need to identify what feels best for you and choose
accordingly. I like both situations and get different things out
of each. I like getting to know people, their children, and
how they cope. I like connecting with people. That's who I
was before Katie's accident and it's who I am now. I simply
prefer certain people now. I am drawn to those who walk this
path and those who choose to walk it with grace and brave
determination.

If you prefer connecting one on one, talk to your friends.
Likely they know someone who knows someone who has
lost a child. Most people are happy to meet, lend an ear, and
connect. Those of us who have lost a child know the pain,
especially in the early days, and want to reach out to others.
We all carry our own suitcase of grief but can share the burden. You are not alone.

Some suggestions for finding assistance:

- Make an appointment with your family doctor if you
  haven't already. If they don't already know what has
  happened, tell them and have a discussion about mental
  health and possible resources. This may or may not
  include medications and referrals to specialists. Explore
  all your options and keep an open mind.

- Start looking for a reputable counsellor, ideally someone who has suffered a significant loss: however, this
  isn't necessary. The counsellor I see has not lost a child
  but we connect very well. If you don't click right away,
  keep looking.

- Seek out bereaved mothers groups online. Try to find a group that resonates with you and your loss. For example, if your child was born into heaven, you might connect best with those who have suffered a stillborn birth or miscarriage. Be open to different kinds of groups and try them all. Online can be one of the more comfortable ways to start with a group. Later, if you are ready, I recommend seeking out a group that meets in person regularly. There is nothing like a real hug from someone who gets it.

- Call a friend. Talk on the phone or invite her over for coffee. You might want to talk about your child and his/her passing, or you may want to hear something different for a while and might like the distraction of hearing about someone else's world. Communicate your needs.

- Reach out to friends and neighbours to assist with errands or meals.

- Ask your friends and family to connect you to other bereaved moms.

- Connect or reconnect with the church if you are feeling the pull.

- Check out your local chapter of Compassionate Friends and make a connection. Go as soon as you are able. As difficult as it is to walk into a new environment, remember that everyone there is travelling this road too and is there to help you.

It's easy to slide deep into the hole of despair and some days it is harder to climb out than others. Please know that there is immediate help if needed. Never hesitate to call emergency services if you are thinking about harming yourself.

If you are in a crisis,
please go to your hospital,
call 911, or
locate a crisis centre in your region.

Check Point
It's time to check in with your healing.
What are two new ways you can find support on your journey
to HEALING?

_____

_____

_____

Road Block
What is standing in your way?

_____

_____

_____

What can you do to remove this barrier?

_____

_____

_____

<u>Keep Going</u>
What are the next steps to making this happen?

_____

_____

_____

What steps can you take this week?

_____

_____

_____

"Many people wonder how I have been able to 'carry on', so to speak. Little do they know that my friendly smile is hiding a shattered heart of a million pieces held together by the love and support of people around me. The compassion of my tribe never goes unnoticed."

~Krista Seip, mother of Deshien, 13 years old

CHAPTER 9

L — Living your Best Life

"I think it's a choice you make on this journey. You choose to go on and you start by putting one foot in front of the other every day. Living my best life came from thinking about how much zest Alyssa had for life. I ask myself how would she be living? And that's the way I try to live myself. Some days you're going to be angry and mad and sad and other days you're going to laugh and you're going to smile.

I think about 2½ years after Alyssa died, I decided it was okay to laugh and not feel guilty about it. This is my journey and no one else's. Living like this makes me feel good and it brings me peace. I think it's a choice to keep going and put a smile on your face and want good things in your life. You have to acknowledge that you deserve to be happy in spite of everything too.

There comes a point when you have to think: I'm going to live for my child that is no longer here. I'm going to live my best life. I am going to take care of myself. I deserve that. After all these years, I can say my heart feels full. It feels happy. It's never going to be completely whole again, but my heart is happy."

~Jill Townshend Lee, mother of Alyssa, 18 years old

L ife as we know it is forever changed. Our hearts and families will never feel complete again. Yet, here we are—living, breathing, and going through the motions. It seems like we claw our way to the top of the hole, only to slide backwards into the darkness again. Goodness knows that grief is work.

Are you living or existing? Living is making future plans, looking forward to things that you love to do or maybe your child loved to do. Living is doing things on your bucket list and connecting with people that matter most to you. Living is moving forward with love in your heart and doing the best you can.

Existing is merely staying alive. Existing means you are lugging that big ugly suitcase around without opening it up to experience all the light and love inside. Merely existing means you aren't interacting much with others and your aim is to just get through the day. When you exist this way there is absolutely no laughing and you wait for the day to pass so that you can go to sleep. We certainly experience this state of existing after our children are gone, especially in the begin-ning. While there will always be days that we simply exist, my hope is that you will experience days of hope and living too.

There were days I almost snapped at people who were laughing in line at the grocery store. Then I heard a wise woman's words. She asked, "How is that serving you?" The answer is that anger doesn't serve us at all. The anger, bitterness, blame, and shame … none of it serves us at all. The same goes for existing in a state of deep sorrow and pain. How does that serve you? It sure doesn't feel good to be there. It doesn't solve anything. It doesn't bring back your child. And most importantly—it sure doesn't honour our children. What do you think your child would say if he or she saw you in 'exist' mode instead of living your best life? I have said from the start—Katie would kick my butt if she saw me wallowing and living with such heaviness. That's not what I'd want for her, so I'm pretty sure she doesn't want me living that way, either.

I'm not the same person I was and never will be. I don't have energy for everything like I used to. Many things are not important to me anymore. However, I want to live for Katie since she didn't get the opportunities that I have. I try to do things that she liked to do and try to enjoy the food she liked. I even went to Sephora one day because I knew she loved it there. It was something I never would have done before, but it made me smile just a little bit to get a makeover that day.

Some people think it's terrible to laugh after their child dies. They worry others might think badly of them, as if they are not honouring their child or mourning the loss like they should. Everyone has their own way of looking at things but think about this: how would you want your child to live if you died? I want my son to live an amazing life. I want him to conquer every goal and dream and have a fantastic time doing it. I want him to laugh, be happy, and surround himself with great people.

I think that's what our kids in heaven want for us, too.

You might be wondering how living and laughing helps with HEALING.

HEALING is about learning to live with grief in one hand and love in the other. The important part of this statement is *learning to live with*. This learning is a process; it's trial and error and it's picking yourself up when you fall to the floor. Every time you pick yourself up, you learn something. You keep getting up so you know you'll keep getting up. If I'm stuck here without Katie, I plan to live an awesome life and I may as well do some things that make me feel good while I am here.

If I am generally easy to be around and can joke about the trivial things, help people out from time to time, then hopefully, people will want to be around me rather than be repelled. Who wants to be around a dark cloud all the time? Yes, we will have our days, weeks, and moments, but if we are like Eeyore all the time, I bet people will stop calling and eventually, not want to be around us.

I need people. I need to talk and I need to talk about Katie, specifically. Maybe you're not like me. If you don't feel like you need people, you can still find a way to live that brings you meaning, if not joy. Maybe you have a garden that you can build up over time that brings meaning and beauty to your life and honours your child. Maybe you can add quirky garden décor and characters that make you smile. Are you starting to see how all the aspects of HEALING come together? Honouring your child, by creating a new garden in their memory, getting out in the fresh air to work in the garden, connecting with a friend over tea while you trade gardening secrets and you start to live a meaningful life. Like I've said, it doesn't have to be a big thing. Start small and follow your heart.

Think of the people that rely on you as well. I wanted to show my son that we could still live and have fun. I didn't want him to watch his mom become a bitter, closed, antisocial woman. Our children model our behaviours in one way or another. Because I want Ryan to laugh and be successful and be surrounded with good people, I want to model those behaviours. We talk about Katie regularly. He knows that I laugh because I'm trying to live. I also don't want to push my son or my husband away by being lost in my grief. I need them and I have worked really hard to keep this little family together, so we carry on and live to honour Katie.

Author Eric R. Maisel writes in a *Psychology Today* article:

> "Loss reminds us that life is short. Use times of loss as an opportunity to reassess your own life, and begin to ask yourself questions about whether you are living a life filled with joy, doing what you love, and making meaning in your life. Begin to live intentionally, consciously choosing how you live your life. View this as a chance to gradually make some changes that allow you to live mindfully and live well.[19]

So the question now is—how do I do that? How do I learn to live again? How do I do things my child used to do knowing they are gone? How do I manage in a group setting without falling apart? How can I live when I can't even breathe?

You're empty and the laughter has gone away. Have you started implementing some of the suggestions from the earlier chapters? A good first step might be to call a friend to go for a walk. You can talk along the way, but get out and enjoy nature, get some fresh air, and some exercise. After your walk, you can enjoy some tea or a healthy smoothie. By reaching out to friends, you are sending a message that you want to start living again. That's a great place to start.

As for the smiling and laughing, you don't have to be the life of the party any time soon and you don't have to be fake. Start with the little things. Try watching a funny sitcom or movie that you or your child loved to watch. Do you have any funny memories of your child that made you laugh? Katie had some really funny sayings and oh my goodness she could rant. In the early days, we would chuckle at some of those memories and my husband even started writing them down. Now when he needs a lift, he pulls up the document on the computer and has a little laugh.

The more people hear you talk openly about your child, the more they will know that it's okay to talk about him or her. Remember, people are walking on eggshells not wanting to hurt you, so most of the time you are going to have to tell them or show them how to act and talk around you by setting the stage.

I try to picture Katie standing beside me and try to always make her happy and proud of what I am doing. I've also heard it said that spirits tend to visit where there is positive energy and I don't know about you, but I love the thought of Katie's spirit visiting often.

By now we have probably all heard the term it's okay not to be okay. It helps to take some of the pressure off and allows us the time we need. But I think we also need to know that it's okay to be okay, too. It's okay to laugh, to say you're doing well, to go to a party, and go on a holiday. Never feel like you shouldn't live because your child died. That's exactly why you need to live.

Ways to start living again:

- Savour simple pleasures (walk through a floral conservatory or where there are flowers and enjoy the scent, or enjoy your child's favourite meal.)

- Practice joy (it may not come easy but give yourself permission and be open to the idea of moments of happiness again.)

- Watch a light comedy on TV, go to a funny movie or watch a DVD that your child liked. Let yourself smile.

- Make a bucket list (you may find your list is different than it was before your child died.)

- Plan a trip. Did your child have a dream-vacation list or goals that they did not accomplish? (You may consider completing those activities in your child's memory.)

- Plan an event or party in memory of your child (if this is too much, invite a few friends over and tell them each to bring something. Be honest and let them know you are trying to take baby steps forward with your HEALING. They will understand if the evening is short.)

- Reflect on your career. Is it time to make changes? (Try not to make any rash decisions in your first year and if financially possible, take as much time off as you need.)

- Plan an afternoon with your children who are alive, ideally one at a time. (Let them know you are still their mom and you love spending time with them.)

- Have a date night with your spouse or partner. (Even a quick dinner out, but go alone. Try to stay connected.)

- Find new activities that bring you pleasure (you might try a Paint Night or take up knitting or Pilates.)

- Take a cooking class (learn to make donuts or poutine or your child's favourite dish.)

- Plan a weekend getaway with your family (it doesn't have to be big or expensive, but a change of scenery and simply being together can be refreshing.)

- Be creative. There is no right or wrong here, but keep finding things that make your heart feel a little bit lighter.

Check Point
It's time to check in with your healing.
What are two new ways you can start living again?

_____

_____

_____

Road Block
What is standing in your way?

_____

_____

_____

What can you do to remove this barrier?

_____

_____

_____

<u>Keep Going</u>
What are the next steps to making this happen?

_____

_____

_____

What steps can you take this week?

_____

_____

_____

"Together we look for the positives and we are very grateful for all the blessings we still have here on this earth. We all try our best to live life to the fullest enjoying slivers of hope and joy—we know that's what Justin would want for us. ... Some days are just easier to do that than others."

~Marlene Lamb, mother of Justin, 25 years old

CHAPTER 10

I — Ideas and Intentions

"I am no longer satisfied to just 'survive' life as I once did. I am no longer able to just bury painful emotions and pretend that it will magically get better someday. I now truly understand that our lives require a lot of work ... I have fully learned that only I am responsible for my own situation and path in life—and indeed, my own happiness. That is not to say that I don't still falter and fall back into old bad habits and thoughts. But now that I have seen this gift that is life so quickly taken away, I am compelled to keep moving forward whenever I stumble ... for if I have learned anything from both (my daughter's) life and her death, it is that love is always within us, around us, and the way through. I often hear other parents faced with the tremendous pain of losing a child ask, "How do I go on?" Many times, both I and others answer, "You just

do; one day or one moment at a time." But the real answer is love.
Our love is what gets us through the darkest moments."

~Maria Kubitz, mother of Margareta, 4 years old[20]

The mind is a very powerful tool. I have experienced this first-hand at many points in my life. On this journey to HEALING, your ideas and intentions can either help you open up your suitcase or keep it zipped up forever. Have you heard the phrase "Whether you think you can or can't, you're right?" Henry Ford made that quote famous and, if you think about it, he's absolutely correct.

The trauma of child loss changes us. It shakes us to the core. How we cope and ultimately learn to carry our suitcases is somewhat dependant on our personality. We are all unique and our dispositions are vastly different, yet there tends to be three main approaches to HEALING that I have encountered on this path: the closed approach, the open approach, and the cautious approach.

The first group has what I call the *closed approach*. A mindset like this can make everything more challenging. Oftentimes, those people have already made up their minds that their life ended when their child died and that nothing will ever help them. And more often that not, they are right. They are right because their mind is closed to the idea that in time, life can be good again.

The second group of people are those with an *open approach*. Everything about them says *this is hard, but I want to find a way*—whether it is losing weight, beating cancer or starting to move forward after child loss. They step up with a strong will, knowing there will be stumbling blocks along the way and are prepared to tackle them. And you know what? Inevitably these people have better outcomes and find peace and HEALING along the way. They think it, see it in their minds, and believe it their hearts. While the idea of HEALING may seem impossible now, I assure you that it is very possible.

The third set of people fall somewhere in the middle, and they use the *cautious approach*. They are unsure about the path that lies ahead of them, want to begin HEALING, and look to others for assistance along the way. These folks usually do pretty well, too. Sometimes you have to start down the road in the direction you want to go. You don't always have to know the details. It's okay to ask for directions as you go. This is where I was in the beginning. I knew I didn't want to be stuck in the pain and blackness of extreme grief and was open to the idea of HEALING, but I was a little lost and needed direction.

Maybe you are someone who is really confused right now and you don't know what to think or do. Or maybe you are thinking you can't fathom the work or pain of trying to move forward. That's quite normal. Just remember, it's all about taking baby steps and making your mind up to *begin* the journey. Once you make the choice, even the smallest steps can help lead to peace and happiness over time.

In the beginning, I truly thought there was no way that I could go on without Katie. While I love my husband and son immensely, her death knocked me to my knees and made me question everything, including my own will to live.

Like you, I felt my chest tightening and my body fighting to function. I thought I was dying. Maybe I was for a while, I don't know. I challenged myself to get through the next five minutes, then the next five minutes, and so on. I thought for sure this was a nightmare I was going to wake up from. But I never did.

At first, my goal was to survive each day. I had no long-term plans other than to get through the day. For the first year or so, my intention was to continue on so that I could help my son get through the worst time of his life. When Ryan got his feet planted underneath him, I really began to focus on my own HEALING. My intention now is to live my best life and help others, but all of this has taken time.

About a year ago, I heard something that made it easier for me to be okay with moving forward (never to be confused with moving on). It went something like this: our grief never changes (like the suitcase), but our lives grow around the grief. This way of thinking removes the pressure to decrease, eliminate, or change our grief. With this in mind, I started looking for a way to start living *with* my grief.

Our thoughts and beliefs influence our behaviour, too. If you think you can rise above tragedy, you will find a way. If you believe that you can find ways to support yourself and your family on this painful journey, you will. If you tell yourself *I can't*, and you don't believe you are capable, chances are you won't. There are many reasons why you may find the concept of a HEALING mindset challenging. It can be incredibly difficult to change your beliefs and thoughts, especially after child loss. However, if you are working with a therapist or psychologist they may be able to assist you with the way you think about HEALING and help you release self-limiting beliefs.

Eddie Lemoine is an expert on the psychology of success. In his book *Bring About What You Think About*, he points out that "every thought you have produces a result; every thought moves you in a particular direction. The thoughts you think are constantly attracting things, situations, people, and health into your life."[21]

You have probably heard the term *energy flows where the mind goes*. So, if you want to begin HEALING and learn to carry your suitcase of grief in a way that gives your life more meaning, you have to want to heal. The more you tell yourself you can do this, the more you will believe it and eventually you will find ways to help yourself.

Other than losing Katie, I have led a fairly blessed life. I had a great childhood and a healthy home where we lived comfortably; I had access to post-secondary education and came out without owing a dime. I married a great guy and was blessed with two fantastic kids. However, amongst these blessings, I have battled depression and anxiety, struggled with the fears of losing my son, and faced uncertainties in my marriage. I've had my fair share of scrapes and bruises along the way. But the biggest hurt I have known is the grief that accompanies child loss.

Of the 50,000 thoughts we have every day, what we think plays a large role in our overall well being. If our thoughts focus on statements like *I'll never be able to do this*, the mind chews on that thought. If you have a self-defeating thought, your mind will go down that road until we tell it to stop or create a new pathway.

Trust me, I don't always think wonderful, encouraging HEALING thoughts. I have had all kinds of negative thoughts about my life and everyone and everything around me. Did I mention I yelled at God? I'm sure I have thought every awful, pessimistic thought there is. But you know what? None of those thoughts helped me or changed the situation.

No amount of agonizing brings back our children. And the amount of pain, angst, and grief we carry is not a sign of how much we love them or miss them. Just because you try to heal your heart and take steps to continue living does not mean you aren't grieving. Please don't ever think this.

I've always looked to and admired those mothers that have their intentions set towards HEALING, no matter how slowly. I've seen these role models collapse, too, but they get up every single time. These resilient women reach out, find the resources they need, and they keep going. This is the path to HEALING that I want to follow.

Everyone is different. Before our kids died we were different, too. Have you noticed how some people can face adversity and seemingly glide through it while others struggle from Day One and never quite seem to get their feet under them again?

Before you lost your child, how did you deal with life when you encountered hard times? How did you handle a bad breakup? How did you manage a poor performance review at work? Maybe you have had to face the loss of someone close before. How did you cope? The reason I ask these questions is because these reactions are what we fall back to when life punches us in the stomach. If we were inclined to retreat into a corner before, that's what we tend to do after losing our kids. If we were more of the proactive type in the past, we may react that way now, too.

The great news is that you can learn how to become more resilient. Being resilient means that you are prepared to work at your grief; it doesn't mean you aren't going to have your gut-wrenching moments. It's all about persevering.

On this journey to HEALING, I think Mahatma Ghandi's words ring true[22]:

Your beliefs become your thoughts,
Your thoughts become your words,
Your words become your actions,
Your actions become your habits,
Your habits become your values,
Your values become your destiny.

Dr. Bruce Lipton is a developmental biologist and author of *The Biology of Belief*. His book outlines the scientific explanation of the body-mind-spirit connection and how our beliefs control our lives.[23] Listen to your gut and follow your heart. Use your mind, your intentions, and your beliefs to heal.

Suggestions that allow you to set your intentions to heal may include the following:

- Start a journal. Let your thoughts go wherever they may. Write down all that is angering you, who upset you, and why you are mad at the universe. But always end your journal entry on a HEALING note. Then make a list of intentions for the week. Set your intentions to let go of all that does not serve you and fill those spots with love, peace, and healing.

- Search out guided meditations about mindfulness and listen to them with an open mind.

- Find a healing intention or mantra that you can repeat daily, write down, and post where you will see it every day. One that resonates with me is:

I don't know what the next minute, day or week will bring, but I will show myself compassion and learn how to live with my new reality.

- Believe that in time, things will get better and your life and love will grow around your grief.

- Start focusing on your child's life not their death. Start a memory journal. Make a list of all the things that make you smile about your child.

- Find your purpose in life. It might be to guide your children through their grief. It might be to help other bereaved mothers. Maybe it is volunteering at the animal shelter. Find something that fills your bucket. It may change over time, but pick one thing and put your energy into that, as you are able.

- Imagine yourself as you want to be. If you want to experience joy again, imagine that. If you want to be able to enjoy your favourite activities again, imagine that. The important part is to believe that this is how you can be.

- Practise building an open attitude. You won't be perfect but keep trying and you will see the changes that take place over time. Keep saying *I can do this. I will do it for my child in heaven. I will do it for my family and I will do it for me.*

Check Point
It's time to check in with your healing.
What are two ways you can set your intentions to HEALING?

_____

_____

_____

Road Block
What is standing in your way?

_____

_____

_____

What can you do to remove this barrier?

_____

_____

_____

Keep Going
What are the next steps to making this happen?

_____

_____

_____

What steps can you take this week?

_____

_____

_____

"The road to healing is definitely a mindset. Your body is only as strong as your mind allows it to be. You can stay in a funk and not move forward ... or you can choose to try and heal by taking measures to help your mind, body and soul."

~ Lorraine Vetter, mother of Michael, 33 years old

CHAPTER 11

N – Nurturing your Soul

"Yoga is a spiritual practice for me, creating the meditative space in which I can be present with myself, drown out the noise in my head and challenge myself in a safe environment. When I was pregnant with my first child 10 years ago, I attended prenatal yoga classes, and used that quiet time to connect with him and my motherhood. Yoga was a safe and comfortable place for me to be. … When my son Norbert was stillborn, I avoided yoga because I associated it with him and his life. … When I was ready to take my healing into my own hands, I started attending yoga classes and was willing to risk being alone with myself. Through the yoga poses and the meditation, I again felt a familiar sensation of calm and grounding that I used to have when practising. I felt that I had finally found a tool that bridged the gap between the 'new' me and the 'old' me."

~Kiley Hanish, mother of Norbert, born into heaven[24]

Taking care of our spirit is equally important as taking care of our physical and mental well being. Yet, we rarely speak about it. But if we ignore working on our spiritual healing, we are not fully supporting our health.

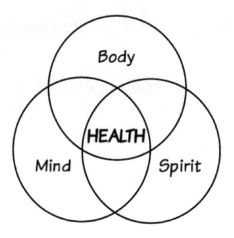

Religion and spirituality are two related yet separate topics. Religion is more defined and formal, praying to a particular Supreme Being often guided by a holy leader. These groups include but are not limited to Christians, Buddhists, Sikhs, Hindus, Muslims, Jews, and others.

Spirituality on the other hand is very open. It is about being open to the notion that we are filled with spirit and that there is a greater force in the universe. Some believe in a spirit world that intertwines with religion. Based on my own experiences, I think these two seemingly different beliefs can co-exist.

On my own journey, I have experienced Katie's spirit more times than I can count. The most memorable moment was the night she died. Lying in bed at 2 a.m. I remember the dancing lights on our bedroom wall that has always been dark at night. When my husband gave in to sleep for a few moments, an outline of two figures appeared in the bedroom doorway. When I quietly asked, "Katie, is that you?" The room was completely enveloped in her perfume for several minutes. Once I made sure that I was lucid and not dreaming, the dancing lights disappeared and the outlines were gone. You may argue that in my anguish, my mind was playing tricks on me. However, that same night at approximately the same time, similar lights appeared to my dad at his condo.

Twenty-four years earlier, I experienced the same kind of visit when my grandmother died. I also believe that my grandmother was the second figure with Katie when she came to me that night. My grandmother brought her to me because she knew I needed that moment with my daughter and that I would be open to the spiritual encounter.

Regarding religion, there tends to be two reactions after the loss of a child. Some people turn away from the church with anger and more questions than answers. And there are others who lean on religion for strength and have renewed faith that is stronger than ever. Both are normal responses and you may bounce between the two.

I feel that any God would be forgiving and understand our questions. If you are experiencing these questions of faith, I encourage you so seek out someone to talk to and do what feels right for you. If you and your partner don't agree on this point, that's okay too. Remember to respect one another during this HEALING process. I found comfort in the church after

Katie's accident and still feel like it's a safe and HEALING place to be.

Prayer was and is something I do with some regularity. It's a chat with my God and the universe. It's an expression of gratitude and an opportunity to look for leadership in tough times. It's a quiet talk that I like to lead with thanks and follow up with a request for strength, hope and HEALING.

Do I know how to pray? Nope. My beliefs are that any Supreme Being understands and is happy to have us connect with Him/Her in any way that is comfortable. I don't like getting caught up in the details. I simply look at it as having a discussion with someone who cares about me and wants to help.

Here's what you can talk to God about if you're not sure where to start. First, pour out your heart. Tell Him about the rawness of your pain, your sadness, anger, and anything else you need to say. Pray for comfort, peace, hope, and healing. You don't need to quote scripture or be well versed in religion at all to have a conversation with God, Buddha, Allah or any other heavenly spirit. Simply start talking and speak from the heart.

You may argue with me, but I feel that praying does not need to be done in a particular building, church, synagogue, or temple. God is always listening and will never turn you away because you are not within the four walls of a place of worship. However, if that is where you are comfortable, that is where you should go. You may also find it helpful to meet with your minister or other spiritual leader, if that's the case.

Meditation is another practice that can help your spirit and regain a sense of calm and HEALING on your journey.

It might seem like an impossible thing to do when you are grieving, but like all the activities suggested in this book, I urge you to keep an open mind and give it a try.

This practice can involve focusing on the breath, may use counting techniques, or it might use the repetition of a mantra. In other words, meditation is not focused on what you are doing as much as turning your attention away from distracting thoughts and focusing on the present moment.

According to WebMD, for the past 30 years, Harvard scientist Herbert Benson, MD has conducted his own studies on prayer. He focuses specifically on meditation, the Buddhist form of prayer, to understand how mind affects body and concludes that "all forms of prayer evoke a relaxation response that quells stress, quiets the body, and promotes healing".[25]

After Katie's accident, I tried everything that I thought might help ease the pain and anxiety I was struggling with. I dabbled with guided meditation and used downloaded voice recordings to help me fall asleep. Not only did I find listening to these guided meditations helpful, but I began to repeat some of the powerful mantras to myself whenever I needed grounding.

I took a fundamental meditation course to better understand the concept. I went to my local yoga studio with a friend for a two-hour introductory class. I had tried meditation before and felt that I couldn't do it, but I signed up anyway. I really liked the yoga instructor that was hosting the workshop and thought she might be able to tell me what I was doing wrong. What I learned is that everyone's mind strays in meditation. The trick is bringing your attention back to the breath or counting. Even if your mind strays 150 times in a 5-minute session, you are meditating.

If you are like me and don't feel capable to meditate on your own, there are numerous guided meditations that you can listen to that will help you through the process. I have even listened to some that guide you along a beach to meet your child on the other side. There are nature-based meditations with the sounds of waves or rain, chakra-based meditations, and some are focused on relaxation or sleep. Try a new one each time and keep track of the ones you like. For me it's all about the voices. Michael Sealey is a hypnotherapist that I find particularly easy to listen to. He has many guided meditations that you can find on the Internet.

Here is a sample meditation for grief by Deepak Chopra, an alternative medicine expert and advocate of the mind-body-spirit connection. Whenever you find yourself feeling overwhelmed with grief for the loss of your child, take a few minutes to sit in stillness by following these meditation steps.

1. Find a comfortable place to sit upright where you won't be disturbed for 15 to 20 minutes. Make yourself comfortable with pillows or a blanket.

2. Begin to breathe slowly and deeply, and place your attention on how you are feeling—both emotionally and physically. Try not to analyze what you are feeling; rather, just be in the experience. Acknowledge your emotions in a gentle and loving way.

3. Imagine the face of the person you are grieving. You may think of it as a manifestation of their spirit or see it as a memory in your mind.

4. Now, consider anything that needs to be said or forgiven and begin to have a conversation with them. Visualize this happening in your mind now. Spend a few minutes saying whatever it is that you need to say from your heart. Then hear them saying whatever

they need to say to you from their heart. Focus on the conversation taking place in a loving and compassionate way—a giving and receiving of open, loving communication with this person.

5. Next, focus on a positive experience you had with this person and immerse yourself in this memory. Relive the happy, fun times and the deep connections that you shared, knowing that these happy memories and moments are what allows grief to release.

6. When you are finished, take a few slow, deep breaths. Sit quietly for a few minutes and bring your meditation to an end. Do this meditation as often as you need to and know that you can always return to this space whenever you want to feel at peace.[26]

Yoga is a total mind-body workout that combines poses with deep breathing, relaxation, and meditation. It is said to help people with a multitude of health problems. Yoga can also be helpful in managing the effects of grief. An instructor trained in grief yoga is able to guide the group through poses to help them cope with the physical and mental challenges of grief.

Grief yoga can help loosen the emotional and physical tightness caused by grief. It is also a healthy way to feel grounded and connected to others travelling this unsure path. Some classes also involve small amounts of sharing, so it might be a good idea to contact the instructor ahead of time to see how the classes are run so you are not caught off guard.

I continue to attend gentle yoga classes and will practise the simple poses at home on difficult days. Grief yoga is a very gentle yoga and anyone can participate, regardless of fitness level. The poses aren't difficult and are focused on opening the body up. There are several grief yoga poses. Three of the more common postures include putting your legs up the wall with your torso on the floor and your arms open wide, lying flat on your back with your arms comfortably at your side and your legs extended and relaxed, and, ironically, a posture called *child's pose*.

The instructors that resonate with me are the ones that speak words of HEALING and encouragement, guide our breathing, and use positive imagery. It's important to keep an open mind and try out several classes and instructors to find the fit that is right for you.

The relaxing aspect of yoga cannot be emphasized enough. If you have been struggling with sleep, you may want to attend a warm yoga class in the evening. Go home and slip into your pyjamas and be ready to have a good night's sleep.

There are some instructors that offer online programming as well, so that might be an option for you. One that I have found (available at the time of printing) is griefyoga.com. Sign up and have online yoga delivered to your inbox.

You can nurture your soul in many ways. You might:

- Attend a church, temple, synagogue, or mosque and connect with a member of the clergy to pray with.

- Ask your local church if they host meetings for bereaved parents.

- Pray to your god, ask for assistance, direction, and strength. Remember, prayer is just a conversation.

- Search out and attend a grief yoga class.

- Alternatively, search the Internet for an online grief yoga class such as GriefYoga.com.

- Consider seeing a psychic, but do your research and ensure they have a good reputation.

- Practise the meditation described in this chapter as outlined by Deepak Chopra.

- Search the Internet for guided meditations. You can search them by topic as well. For example, search 'guided meditation for sleep' or 'Michael Sealey guided meditation'.

Check Point
It's time to check in with your healing.
What are two ways you can nurture your soul?

_____

_____

_____

Road Block
What is standing in your way?

_____

_____

_____

What can you do to remove this barrier?

_____

_____

_____

<u>Keep Going</u>
What are the next steps to making this happen?

_____

_____

_____

What steps can you take this week?

_____

_____

_____

"I needed faith to survive. I needed to believe that my son was okay and was continuing his life in another form ... I know that there is a purpose for me through this tragedy, I am just not sure what it is yet."

~Angie Langridge, mother of Layne, 14 years old

CHAPTER 12

G — Gratitude

"Shortly after Stephen's death, I told my son we would need to find 'one little thing' each day to hold on to help us when we felt sad. I knew that I needed to look for those little things to take comfort in the dark days of mourning. And, to my surprise, I found countless things to be grateful for each day. It created a shift in my thinking, in my grieving, and in my life. I am thankful for Stephen … I am so, so thankful for him, and for the twenty-three years I did have with him. I cannot imagine where I would be in life without his influence. He changed me from the moment I looked into those eyes of his, those old and knowing eyes. He changed me with his life and with his death. I am thankful for him and for all that he gave me and continues to give me through my reflection. I am thankful that so many others were touched by his life as well. I am humbled, silenced, and speechless, by the people who have and continue to reach out, simply to say he changed them, he affected them, and he loved them and took care of them just how they needed. Every mother should be

so lucky to hear the words I have about their child. … I am grateful, no matter how hard it is for me to say."

> ~Kelly S. Buckley, mother of Stephen, 23 years old, and author of Gratitude in Grief[27]

My experience with gratitude began about five minutes after the police officer and coroner visited our home the night Katie died. I remember being thankful that she died instantly. I remember being thankful that she didn't have any passengers. I remember wanting to thank the entire emergency crew that was at the scene. What? Who is grateful within minutes of learning that their child has died? I guess that would be me, and I really can't tell you why these things ran through my head, but it's the truth.

I remember being in the thick of early grief and dealing with other family issues and thinking I was going to explode. All I saw was the growing pile of negatives in my life. I labelled it all *bad* and I dwelled on every rotten detail about every rotten situation. I was angry with everyone for being in this situation and I was angrier with certain people for making it even more difficult. That negativity started rolling over into every part of my life. I couldn't look at someone on the street without thinking angry and negative things about them. I snapped at my husband because everything that came out of his mouth made me mad. The flowers that were starting to die upset me because all I saw was death.

I saw, felt, and experienced everything that my mind told me to. I was so focused on the anger and extreme sadness over losing Katie that I could not see anything good around me. One day, I said to my husband, "We need to start talking about things differently. We need to choose our words more carefully and we need to believe that there is good in our lives."

It was hard. It was so hard. But if I found one good thing every day, it helped. Once I started that practice, it seemed like things got a wee bit better. The people and situations that challenged me became less of a concern because I focused on the good things, no matter how insignificant they seemed. I started to praise my son instead of nag him. I chose to find the positive wherever I could. When I crawled into bed at night, I counted all my blessings. In the beginning I struggled with this, but in time my list grew.

Gratitude and Grief, by Kelly S. Buckley, was one of the first books I read. My concentration was terrible in those early days, but her message really spoke to me, so I persisted and read a little bit every day. I really identified with her journey and felt connected by her experience. Kelly's idea of finding one little thing to be grateful for every day seemed achievable.

When you start looking for the good, you see the good. I started seeing the incredible beauty in the sunrise and sunset. I saw hope in the bunnies huddled together under the shrubs. I found peace in the early morning quiet and I found love in the kind actions of others.

It's easy to be grateful when things are going well. It's easy to be grateful when you get a promotion, or when your husband surprises you with a bouquet of flowers, or when you arrive safely at your destination in a snowstorm. Since gratitude and grief are nearly opposites, it stands to reason that they seem incompatible.

The power of gratitude after child loss is actually about focusing on the love and beauty of our child's life, not their death. I know it can seem utterly impossible to think beyond what has happened and the long road ahead. Trust me when I say that gratitude is so incredibly powerful that it can literally flip a switch in your brain and make you feel like you will survive.

There is science that supports the fact that gratitude plays a role in our well being. A study done by researchers Nathan Greene and Katie McGovern suggests that there is a positive correlation between gratitude and improved well being after traumatic loss. This study also suggests when gratitude is absent, there tends to be a greater likelihood of depression. The researchers go on to say that participants who practise gratitude report a greater appreciation for family and friends and believe that life is precious.[28]

Research shows that gratitude reduces the negative emotions that prevent us from HEALING. This means that anger, jealousy, bitterness, and regret diminish, while sleep and stress improve. Being grateful also gives us a sense of power. It is our choice after all. When we are making the choice to be grateful, we become more resilient.[29]

Gratitude can be a tough pill to swallow, especially in the beginning, but it changes our focus. It's a skill that takes time to develop, but is worth the effort. Practice will make gratitude habitual and seem easier over time. Thankfulness actually lightens the weight of your suitcase and makes it much easier to carry. It's another tool for your grief toolbelt and it does make things a wee bit easier.

On my own road, I have experienced two different kinds of gratitude—past gratitude and present gratitude—and they both become easier with time and practice. As my gratitude muscle grows stronger, I find myself able to look at things differently.

Past gratitude is merely being happy for the past—not Katie's accident, but the 17½ years that I had with Katie. I worked part-time as much as possible throughout her life and am grateful for that decision. I'm also so very happy that she was a healthy girl and that every minute leading up to her accident she was able to live a great life and we were able to travel and make wonderful family memories.

Present gratitude is something that I practised most in the early days. I would lay in bed, unable to sleep, and try to pass the time. I'd make a mental list of things I was grateful for. Some days it was pretty basic. I was grateful for a roof over my head, food in the fridge, and a warm bed. Usually I'd find a few other things to be grateful for, like the white feather I found on the couch with no explanation or the numerous other signs I seemed to be receiving. Then my mind would wander down that path, but it was a positive path because it was based on gratitude.

I would find myself looking for things to be grateful for, so that each night my list wasn't the same as the night before. I remember seeing a goofy black lab frolicking in the snow. He was chasing snowflakes and rolling around with such delight. His happiness was contagious and for a brief moment I smiled at his joy. I made a mental note to add the happy dog to my daily gratitude list that night. Every day, I challenged myself to find more things that I was thankful for. Ultimately, this encouraged me to look for the good in every day.

If you haven't already, this may be the perfect time to open up your suitcase of grief. Remember, if you peak inside without opening it all the way, it will still appear dark inside. Open your suitcase to discover all the love and beauty that your child has left for you. Open your suitcase and open your heart.

Here is a list of things that I am grateful for (listed in no particular order):

- 17½ years with Katie, an amazing and healthy daughter. Our time together was filled with wonderful holidays, laughing, great talks, dance competition trips, and so much more (not everyone gets 17½ years with their child).

- My son. Where oh where would I be without this boy in my life? He has taught me so much.

- My husband. I am grateful to have a supportive shoulder to lean on.

- The ability to take a paid leave from work and a supportive employer that allowed me to take all the time I needed.

- A healthy heart that kept beating even though I thought it would surely stop.

- True friends, both new and old, who continue to hold me up and check in.

- The blue sky and the shining sun for the days that my soul needs a lift.

- A healthy body that I can use every day to help me on my road to HEALING.

- Knowledge of good nutrition to support my arduous journey.

- A bank account that allowed us to take short trips during the first year which helped us get our footing and learn how to be a family of three.

- Katie's friends who stayed close and shared personal stories about her.

- The group of amazing bereaved mothers who held their arms out and held me up when they were dealing with their own losses.

- The handful of dedicated and tireless teachers who never gave up on my son when he didn't know how to handle his grief.

- The angels above who have protected my son, my husband, and me from further hurts.

- An incredibly mild winter the year that Katie died. It allowed me to get outside almost every day that winter. I did a lot of walking, praying, and crying on those winter days.

- The feathers and other signs that have been so plentiful, giving me hope and helping me believe that there is life after death.

Ways that you can implement more gratitude into your HEALING journey:

- Start a gratitude journal. Start by listing three things that you are thankful for. Leave it on your nightstand so that you write in it every night.

- Create a list of what you are thankful for, like I have done. Include everyone and everything you can think of.

- Practice Kelly S. Buckley's "one little thing" approach. Find one positive thing each and every day.

- Think of the people you are grateful for and why.

- Reflect back on the time you spent with your child. What are your favourite memories? Maybe it was feeling their movements when you were pregnant or a family holiday. Make a list.

- Join a gratitude group on social media. Can't find one? Start one. A dear friend challenged herself to 100 days of gratitude and shared her thoughts on social media. I looked forward to reading her post each day.

- Start saying a sincere thank you to one person every day and why you are thankful for them.

- Start practising random acts of kindness. It really is a great feeling. Buy someone's coffee, donate your time, help an elderly person, etc.

- Look for the hidden lessons in life's challenges. That speeding ticket was a message to slow down.

- Volunteer somewhere that holds meaning to you. Giving back is being grateful.

- Make a commitment to stop looking at all the negatives for a week and choose to find all the positives instead.

- Make gratitude part of mealtime and encourage everyone at the table to share something that they are thankful for or the best part of their day.

- Share gratitude by posting on social media. Ask others what they are thankful for and in turn share what you are grateful for.

Check Point
It's time to check in with your healing.
How will you practice gratitude on your journey to HEALING?

_____

_____

_____

Road Block
What is standing in your way?

_____

_____

_____

What can you do to remove this barrier?

_____

_____

_____

Keep Going
What are the next steps to making this happen?

_____

_____

_____

What steps can you take this week?

_____

_____

_____

"As I sit here with mixed emotions about another first without Kailynn, I realize that I do feel thankful even in my grief. I am thankful that she chose to call me mommy, I am thankful for the 17 great years that I had with her. I am thankful that I have the memories that I hold dear."

~ Sandra LaRose, mother of Kailynn, 17 years old

PART 4

The Plan

CHAPTER 13

Your Path

"Following several miscarriages, I delivered a stillborn baby boy, Samuel. When I held this child in my arms saying both my hello and my goodbye on the very same day, my heart broke so much that I truly believed it was beyond repair. It took years for me to regain even a small amount of trust in life again.

That all changed ... when the phone rang. My firstborn son died unexpectedly of a massive heart attack at the early age of forty-two.

As hard as this may sound, the truth is that bringing hope back into our lives becomes a choice that we must make. Many parents will turn away from this thought saying we are denied hope because our child is no longer here. Every reason for living has been taken away. Many have erringly convinced themselves that they do not deserve to feel the blessing of hope again, so they give up on life...

When we think of hope as a choice, it becomes something that feels tangible and achievable. Hope becomes a goal to work towards.

Hope is a challenge to accept the reality of our loss and to hold fast to the belief that life will again be worth living...

I have travelled this path of child loss several times over now, and I can say to you with all sincerity and truth that there is hope beyond the heartbreak."

~ Clara Hinton, mother of Samuel born into heaven and Mike 42 years old, and author of Child Loss[30]

I hope that you have found some strategies to help you on your journey to HEALING, and that you took time at each Check Point to weigh in on how you are feeling about your HEALING. Did you write down specific steps that you can take?

Journey to HEALING was designed as a reference book that you can refer back to often. As our journeys change over time so do our needs. You may feel that you can only manage one tiny step right now or you may be feeling like you are ready to take a bigger stride and delve into your HEALING. Either way, the only way you are going to change the way you feel is by changing your thoughts and actions. Once you make the decision to begin the journey, you will be headed toward a place that honours your child and brings you peace.

While these tools do not eliminate your sadness and sense of loss, they can help you move in the direction of HEALING. This might seem scary. Be open and be brave. Change comes from doing things differently and HEALING comes from taking action.

On my own path, I have found that each day, week, and month can be different which is why I encourage you to find as many tools as you can for your HEALING journey. Some days one thing may help and other days it may not, so it's good to have a number of options.

This is your path. No one else's. Find what works for you. Take baby steps and move as slowly as needed.

If you picked up this book, you have a desire to begin HEALING. In the last several chapters, you have learned ways to help ease your pain and find peace while you journey through grief. The big question now is how you will implement these suggested strategies.

First, you need to love yourself enough to make changes and know that you deserve to find happiness again. Accept that you will falter along the way. We all do. The key is to keep getting up and continuing on your path to HEALING. Keep putting one foot in front of the other.

You may struggle at times, so I think it's helpful to know how to handle those situations and how to get yourself back on track. Let's say you have a really, really bad week and find yourself unable to cope. Perhaps you cannot get out of bed, have shut out your support people, and are struggling with profound grief. Take your moment, feel the intense sorrow and pain, but know that you aren't going to stay there.

When you are ready to get up and take another step forward, you need to say "Enough. This is not helping me." Take ten breaths to reset yourself. Next, choose a new behaviour, skill or strategy that you have learned here and put it into action as soon as possible.

In the above situation, you might get out of bed, shower, and put on clean clothes. You could call one of your trusted support people and ask her to stop by for a visit. If your friend is coming by, ask her to bring some peppermint tea and a fruit tray. On the really horrible days you may be capable of only one of these actions, but have a plan in your back pocket for when these times happen. Because they will.

On my worst days, I put my shoes and jacket on and go for a walk by myself. That is how I reset. The fresh air almost always makes me feel better. Find your thing; that one thing that can help you switch gears. Maybe it's calling someone or sitting in your child's room with a journal or listening to their favourite music. Find your reset button and be prepared to utilize it often, especially in the beginning.

Now let's talk about how you can use these tools and strategies on your journey. You have a few options. You can start implementing one strategy per week. I suggest starting with honouring. I have found this one to be the easiest. Go back to your Check Point for Chapter 6 and note one easy and one challenging way you would like to honour your child. Focus on that for one week. Challenge yourself to do those particular activities (at least in part) each day. Another option might be picking one thing from each of the seven HEALING chapters and posting the list somewhere that you will see it daily, like on the refrigerator. Try to choose a different activity each day. You will get in the habit of working on your HEALING each day.

People usually find that creating a new habit is easiest if they dedicate time either at the beginning of the day or the end of the day. Let's say you would like to create a memory book. You might spend 30 minutes each evening finding photos for your book. When you get to the chapter on exercise and self care, you might find you have more energy in the mornings and will plan to wake up a few minutes early to do yoga and make a healthy smoothie before your day gets started. Set aside 30 minutes every day, either morning or evening, and schedule your HEALING time. Trust me: if you don't do this the time will slip by and you won't work on your HEALING. Take a moment and make that time commitment now.

After health coaching for several years, I have found that those who are most successful with change do four things to get on and stay on the right track. First, they visualize how much better their life will be with the new habits. They replace the words "I can't" with "I can and I want to." Next, they tell people about their plans. This creates some level of accountability. And last, they connect with like-minded people who want to create similar kinds of changes in their lives. Online fitness challenges are a good example of this. They have their own online group and post about their workouts, how much weight they have lost, and so on. They also post about their struggles and their bad days. The other members in the group invariably pick them up, encourage them, and support them on their journey.

I haven't found a HEALING group with accountability, so I created one that offers support and encouragement. It's a group for bereaved moms like you and me who want to take the steps towards HEALING and want the added companionship and accountability. Go to https://www.facebook.com/LisaKBoehmSupport then click the blue *visit group* button. You will be asked to answer a couple of questions and then you will be added to my child loss support group.

Your HEALING is in your hands. Be strong and take your first step. You are not alone. I am right here walking beside you.

"With hard work and reflection, I am starting to feel hope. I will learn to remember my son's life rather than the tragedy of his death."

~ Venessa Vogel, mother of Conal, 19 years old

PART 5

The Journey

CHAPTER 14

Road under Construction

"As time goes by, I handle things differently than I used to. It depends on how I'm feeling that day. Sometimes a trigger can send me upstairs to cry and some days the same thing is okay. Music can be a trigger for my husband and me. For him it's the Bryan Adams' song Heaven *and for me it's Aerosmith's* Dream On *because it was always on the radio when we were driving back and forth to the hospital. Sometimes it's hard to hear and other times, it's okay.*

Back to school is tough. Tyler had just started kindergarten when he was diagnosed with DPIG (a rare pediatric brain tumour—diffuse intrinsic pontine glioma). Watching the rest of the world keep moving while my child was never able to do those things has been hard. Every year, all these kids are a year older and experiencing all that the world has to offer. The holidays and Christmas are triggers too.

My son was born ten days before Christmas, so it's kind of a double whammy. It hits so hard at that time of the year. Family holidays in general are tough. There's always someone missing.

Tyler never learned how to ride his bike, so springtime can be a challenge for me. I tried to help him learn the summer before, but he didn't get it. Looking back now, I think maybe he had double vision and balance issues already. But when everyone's outside playing, I know my child is missing. It always hurts, but I keep going. It's a choice to move forward—you just have to."

~Kelly Puetz, mother of Tyler, 6½ years old

It seems that around every bend in the road is a trigger. Sometimes you can see them coming, and other times they broadside you. A trigger is an event or situation that stirs up feelings of deep grief and can send you right back to a moment of raw and extreme sadness.[31] It might be someone who looks like your child; it might be the scent of their perfume, or their favourite song. I remember hearing John Lennon's song *Imagine* for the first time in a coffee shop. That was Katie's favourite song. It almost brought me to my knees.

Obvious triggers are the birthdays and angel anniversaries that we face every year. We see them coming and can hunker down to weather the storm. We can plan events if that makes our hearts a wee bit lighter. We can book the day off of work and stay in bed. We can prepare for those days to a certain degree. It doesn't diminish the storm, but we can batten down the hatches and prepare for the pounding surge.

I have found that it's the unseen triggers that can be the toughest. My son's high school graduation was a day that I had planned out for six months. My husband, son, and I awarded three scholarships in Katie's honour. I knew being on stage in front of a large crowd wasn't going to be an easy thing to do, but I was prepared and did fine. I think I even smiled at each of the recipients and sincerely wished them well.

What I didn't prepare for was the moment my son received his diploma. I was a disaster, completely and utterly overcome with emotions. Reality hit me hard. My son had finished high school and was transitioning into adult life, something Katie never got to do. She never got to graduate or pursue her dreams.

The fact is we cannot prepare for every scenario and every possible trigger. We don't know what's going to blindside us on a particular day. The same thing may be okay on one day yet be devastating on another. Triggers will be lifelong companions and we have to learn to cope with them.

I am learning that I need time to myself before and after big events like Katie's birthday, angel anniversary, and days like my son's grad. I need to book my schedule accordingly. There is no gold medal for pushing through any of it, either. I know myself and I honour the hard days as much as I honour the HEALING days. I allow myself a bad day or two, crying and all the rest of it, but I choose not to stay there. I don't want to stay there either. I don't like anything about that place. It scares me and I think it scares the people around me.

The lure to mask the pain can be tempting. Unhealthy means of coping can quickly lead to big problems. Some turn to alcohol, some shopping, others turn to affairs, drugs, food, or burying themselves in their careers. These are all ways of avoiding the pain and the HEALING. I have observed it with my own eyes. Grief is always there, waiting. Eventually it will catch up with you.

Grief is something you have to go through and learn to live with. If you constantly shove it down and continue to suppress the pain, it will manifest in you mentally, physically, and emotionally. No one needs any more pain and suffering. The only way to survive this is to have some healthy coping skills that truly help you on this painful path.

If you think you or a loved one is coping with excessive use of substances or coping in an unhealthy way, please reach out. This is a cry for help. It can be a tough conversation, but when you reach out you are telling that person that you love them and are concerned.

At this point it's worth noting that as parents, we model behaviours for our children from day one. No matter their age, our children are very impressionable. Our living children are watching us and need us more than ever.

If we turn to unhealthy ways of coping, there is a good chance that they will too. If we are highly reactive and lash out at others on this journey, so will they. If we keep talking about our child in heaven and make death okay to talk about, then they will do the same. I know just getting up some days can be a challenge, but do try to think of your living children on this journey too. They need you, no matter how old they are, and they look to you for guidance.

I read many, many books as I prepared to write this one. I read some great books, some not-so-great books, and a few that I will never forget. One book called *Beyond Tears; Living after Losing a Child*, interviewed mothers who had lost children. At the end of this book, the now-grown-up siblings were interviewed. Some of the grown children felt as though their own parents had forgot them and believed their own life wasn't as valuable as the child who died. How heartbreaking. Please take time for your surviving children. Please remember they are hurting just like you. If you are unable to support them right now, ask family or friends for assistance.

The secret to survival isn't really a secret at all. Survival comes from riding out the storm and choosing to get your feet back under you. The storms will always come and you must continue to find the strength to manage them. We all agree that time does not heal. However, time does bring strength and a sense of knowing. Each time you survive a storm surge, you have the knowledge and the experience of getting through so you know when the next one hits, that you can get up once again.

I encourage you to hold on and be open to a lifetime of HEALING. Some will tell you that the first year is the hardest. They are right. Some might tell you the second year is the hardest. They are also right. The third and fourth years? They too might be the hardest. I've come to the conclusion that this journey doesn't get easier. We get stronger. We learn how to carry our suitcase of grief. We learn how to cherish our child's life and not focus on their death.

Not only do we have to choose the journey to HEALING, but we have to realize that to feel differently we have to do things differently. What's that saying? Insanity is doing things the same way over and over again, but expecting a different outcome.[32] Therefore, if your current approach is not helping you cope or manage your grief, it may be time to try some new strategies.

Keep this book and website printout (available at https://www.lisakboehm.com/your-healing-pathway) handy. Refer to it often and challenge yourself to keep going. Even if things are going reasonably well, I suggest you explore new ways to help you on this road. Remember that HEALING is a journey, not a destination. You may find that yoga really helps you for a while, and then it may stop being as effective as it once was.

There was a time when I was using all of my tools in a single day. I would go for a walk, connect with another mom, meditate, go to yoga, journal, chat out loud with Katie, and work on her memory book. Some days that still wasn't enough, so I wrapped myself in Katie's sweaters, sat in her room, and cooked her favourite meals.

Use this book to help you when you are stuck. Refer back to the lists and strategies and use them often. HEALING only happens when you work at it.

My wish is that you begin to see past the towering mountain in front of you and focus on the flowers and beauty along its path. Reach out to others and allow your heart to heal. Your dedication to HEALING will make this journey much easier for you. This I promise you.

This may be the most difficult journey of your life. It's terrifying and incredibly challenging, but you can do it. You are about to realize how capable and resilient you are.

"You need bruises to know blessings and I have known both."

~Frances Shand Kydd, mother of Princess Diana,
36 years old[33]

CHAPTER 15

Take the Scenic Route

"After hitting an all-time low, I realized I might have decades left to live, and as difficult as it might be to move forward without my daughter, I knew I needed to strive to find happiness again.

As the pain softened, and I began searching, I found it in the little things I had once taken for granted. I found happiness in every single milestone that I've been able to experience with my four other children … I found it in my husband's laugh, which had been stifled by grief for far too long.

…I'm definitely still Preslee's mom, it just looks differently than it used to. My little girl continues to teach me that life doesn't have to be perfect for it to be wonderful.

Though motherhood hasn't quite turned out the way I thought it would, you better believe I still have goals and aspirations; they're just a little different than they were seven years ago. Most of my dreams have a deeper meaning now, which stems from everything Preslee has taught me.

I'm striving to live a life worth living and helping as many people as I can along the way. So I guess you can say Preslee is still at the center of it all, and I might just be the luckiest person there is, because I'm the only person she calls mom."

~Ashley Sullenger, mother of Preslee, 18 months old[34]

I chose to live and travel the road to HEALING initially for my son. But, over time, I continue on this path because it feels right. And sometimes I find another feather and hear a voice over my shoulder: "You've got this, Mom." I truly believe this is how Katie—and all of our children—wants us to live.

It's easy to get sucked into the thinking, "But my child isn't here to enjoy all these things. How can I go on enjoying life?" I like to think of it as enjoying life *for* Katie—including the things she didn't get to do or those that she loved to do.

What's your reason to keep going? You may not think you have one, but you do. If you allow the layers of pain and hurt to fall away for a moment, you will know what your purpose is.

Do you have a message to share with the world? A passion to see safety regulations improved? Maybe you have a voice to bring awareness and change to bullying or mental health issues that will positively impact the lives of other children? What about drugs? Perhaps your passion is joining forces with organizations to help promote education. You might be the person with the voice that saves a life.

Find your purpose, find your path. Honour your child in heaven.

You now have the tools and strategies to keep you going. Let your purpose and passion be the spark you need to keep going.

Know that this road will always be rocky. There will be triggers all along the way. Your new reality will always be a balancing act between grief and sadness and times of peace and happiness. Grab hold of those moments of peace and happiness and squeeze every ounce out of them. You deserve them and you should enjoy them.

I would sell my soul to the devil himself to have Katie back. Yet, I feel like I have learned so much. I named this book *Journey to HEALING* because it is a brutal road, harder than any of us could imagine. I struggle to say that there is good in Katie's death or any child's death, but I will say that I have experienced so much transformation and learning which has affected all areas of my life.

Katie will forever be woven into the fabric of my life and she will continue to guide me from beyond. While not a day goes by without some pain and sadness, wishing she were here with me, Katie's death has taught me more than I ever thought possible.

Here is what I have learned:

- Life is short. It is a gift not to be wasted. The days pass no matter what. We can pass the days in pain or in peace.

- It's okay to cry. This is our body's way of releasing pain. We don't always have to be strong. Own your feelings; lean into them. Stay there as long as you need, but don't stay there forever. Crying is a human reaction and it's healthy. We must grieve in order to move forward.

- It's all right to lean on others. We need each other. We can't travel this path alone.

- People want to help. Help them help you by saying yes. Try to be patient when they stumble on clichés and don't know what to say. Everything comes with good intentions even if the execution seems hurtful.

- It's okay to laugh on this journey. Katie had the most infectious laugh and laughed loud and strong. Laugh with warm memories and love in your heart.

- Love is the greatest gift. Love everyone and everything. Make every decision based on love and see how your life changes.

- Cherish the good memories. You will carry them with you forever.

- By holding on to grief, we are focusing on our child's death. When we work on our HEALING, we are focusing on their life.

- Nothing in life is permanent. Enjoy what you can when you can. It can all change in a heartbeat.

- You are not to blame for your child's death. Blame and guilt will prevent you from seeing the beauty in your child's life.

- Our loved ones are only a whisper away. Heaven is not way up in the sky, it is right beside us. Our children are with us every step of the way. Although they are no longer with us physically, they live on in our hearts, our minds, and our dreams.

- Speak up for what's important, do the right thing, and offer a hand up to those who need it. HEALING can come from helping too. Actions really do speak louder than words.

- Being miserable, bitter, and angry does not change a thing. In time it may push away all the good in your life.

- Living and loving are choices and they fill our lives with meaning and hope.

- Find your tribe. Choose to be with people who lift you up, inspire you and encourage you to be okay. Look for a supportive group of mothers that are the best fit for you and start lifting each other up.

- Katie's death gave me the opportunity to take a good look at my life. It was a wake-up call I wouldn't wish on anyone, but it's also been the defining moment in my life. I have clarity about who I want to be and whom I want to spend my time with. The petty things are just petty things now. I cherish my family and will never let them go out the door without an "I love you" or a hug.

- Death is a taboo subject in our society and it's not helpful for HEALING. Let's talk about it and let's change the way we deal with loss.

- Allow yourself to find peace by acknowledging your grief. You will learn to build your life around your grief, just as you will learn to carry your suitcase of grief.

- There is a life beyond your loss and, in time, it can be filled with joy and laughter, if you let it. But it's work. *Hard* work.

- Katie's death was a reminder to go after what really makes me happy and I am so thankful for that. I always wanted her to have an amazing life and she did for 17½ years. I will make sure that I will enjoy mine as much as I can—for her.

- There is hope. Every day might not be good but there is good in every day.

- Love never dies. We grieve the loss of our children because we miss everything about them and mourn the loss of their future and our future with them. Grief is love.

- If you can't see the good, make the good. Start a movement, change laws, have safety lighting installed along the road, plant a tree, or create a scholarship. Grieving mothers are a force to be reckoned with. We can turn loss into legacy.

- The suffering and the sorrow will always be with you, but it is your choice if you let it run and ruin your life.

- I know deep sorrow and because of that I know joy. When you have experienced pain so horrific, you will see that the sun shines brighter on a summer day and that each day is a gift. After experiencing such devastation, we live from a deeper place. This is also how grief changes us. I am grateful for the joy, no matter how it comes.

- Be fully present in all aspects of life. Don't spend your life with your head buried. Put down your phone. Connect with people.

- Take loads of pictures and videos. Back them up. Organize them. They are more valuable than you will ever know especially when they are all that you have of the person you love.

- Take nothing for granted. *Ever.*

- Take the scenic route when you can. Find the beauty and enjoy the sights and find the things that make you smile. Take your time. Only you can travel this road.

I am a survivor and stronger than I ever imagined. I hope I never have to face anything like losing Katie again, but I know if I do, I will survive. I have already endured the worst that life can throw at me. I am grateful to walk this path with a dedicated husband who stood by my side and held me up.

I have my two children to thank as well—my son who walks beside me and my daughter who guides me every day. You are both the best gifts I have ever been given.

"The journey of a thousand miles begins with one step."

~Lao Tzu, Chinese philosopher[35]

Pick up your suitcase firmly in your hand and take that step with me. You are not alone. We will walk it together.

You Can Shed Tears That She is Gone

You can shed tears that she is gone,

Or you can smile because she lived.

You can close your eyes and pray that she'll come back,

Or you can open your eyes and see all she's left.

Your heart can be empty because you can't see her,

Or you can be full of the love you shared.

You can turn your back on tomorrow and live yesterday,

Or you can be happy for tomorrow because of yesterday.

You can remember only that she is gone,

Or you can cherish her memory and let it live on.

You can cry and close your mind, be empty and
turn your back,

Or you can do what she'd want: smile, open your eyes,
love and go on.

By David Harkins

For the Supporters

"Remember that grief is indefinite. For the bereaved, it contin-ues well past when people remember the tragedy. When the funerals pass and the visitors go home, life gets harder, heavier, and much more real for a long period of time. There is no linear progression, no predictable stages of grief. People often apologize for bringing up Sebastian. You don't need to apologize; you don't need to feel awkward. You are acknowledging my loss and our perpetual state of grief."

~Andrea Schick, mother of Sebastian, 4½ years old

If you are a friend of a bereaved mom, family, or even an acquaintance, please be patient with us. We may look the same to you, but we are very, very different now. We are fragile and need lots of kindness and patience. Please know that there is no timeline to HEALING, that HEALING is the choice of the bereaved. It is not your choice or your timeline. We have different wants and needs than we had before our child died and those change over time. No two people grieve the same. Good communication, like other areas of life, is paramount.

Sometimes, as a supporter, it is hard to know what to do or say. I've been there as we all have. I have compiled this list with the help of other grieving mothers. These are the things that we have found helpful and those that were not.

To help you best support a bereaved mother consider the following:

PLEASE:

- Acknowledge our child's passing. Say something and do something. Remember our children, say their name. We won't be upset. We might cry at hearing their name, but it brings us joy. Share memories, pictures, anything at all.

- Understand that this journey is a balancing act for us, grief in one hand and moments of peace in the other. Know that we can experience both and some days we need more patience and support than others. Our grief never goes away.

- Know that our lives will never, ever be the same. It's not only the loss of our child that we grieve; it's the loss of all future moments with our child. We mourn the big things like lost future weddings and grandchildren, and the smaller reminders such as the empty chair at the kitchen table.

- Be there for the long haul. We need you and your support forever. While your life goes back to normal after the funeral, ours is silent and lonely. We need you to stay in touch and reach out after the funeral is over for the days, months and years to come. Visit, send texts, and emails. It all helps.

- Encourage conversations and memories about our children. Include them in the conversation.

- Listen. *Really listen.*

- Write down our child's birthday and date of death on a calendar and send a message or card on those days. You won't make us sad by reminding us that our children are no longer here. We will never forget that, but by remembering and saying our child's name you will warm our heart. We are all scared that our child will be forgotten. Please remember them.

- Be gentle and considerate. Ask if we want to talk about what happened. Let us talk, rant, and scream. Listen and acknowledge our pain. Do not offer suggestions unless you have walked this path. *Please* stay away from the clichés. (See below)

- At least two days every year, we need some grace: our child's birthday and their anniversary will always be days that we need the most understanding. However, every holiday no matter how big or small, is difficult.

- If you want to take food to the bereaved family, use disposable containers that are labelled and ready to freeze. Having to find the energy to return items can be overwhelming. Better yet, divide into smaller serving sizes and label. Another good idea is restaurant gift cards that can be used when all the casseroles and food are gone.

- Keep checking in, considerately. We may turn you down 20 times but keep asking. Give us space but keep letting us know you are thinking of us and wanting to visit when it feels right for us. Invite us out, or ask to stop by. Keep calling and texting.

- Step in and step up graciously. Don't say, "If there's anything you I can do, just ask." We do not have the energy or the forethought to do that. Bring a meal or a cup of tea. Arrange to take our kids to activities or take care of our pets.

- Understand that grief is complex and difficult for us to understand too. Know that you can't fix this.

Please SAY:

- I am so sorry.

- I don't know what to say but I am heartbroken for you.

- This must be so difficult for you. Does it help to talk about your child?

- This is so unfair and I don't understand why it has to be this way.

- I haven't been through anything like this but I want to support you.

- I wish I knew the answers, but I really don't know why this happened.

- I don't know what to say or how to best support you, but I am going to stay close. You may have to give me some pointers but I want to support you.

- If you'd like to talk about your child, I would love to listen.

- I have a wonderful memory about your child. Do you mind if I share it with you?

- If you are sending texts or emails, sending a message that simply says *hugs* followed by heart emojis can make us feel loved and let's us know you are thinking about us.

- I would like to help you as much as I can.

- I'm going to the grocery store. Do you have enough milk? Or bread? Kleenex? (Ask direct questions.)

- I would like to watch your kids for you so you can have a nap or have some time to yourself. When would that work for you?

- I think of you and your child so often.

Be aware of your wording as well. If a child has died from suicide, it can be very hurtful and aggravating to hear words like, "I could have killed him" or "Hang in there." Listen to the words the mother uses and use that language. If you aren't sure, ask. I'm sure that your concern will be met with gratitude.

True support does not mean you are there to cheer us up. We need to talk about our child's death over and over again. Other times we may need to be quiet. The best support is not related to what you say, but rather your presence and how effectively you listen. That is the greatest gift you can give us. If you really don't know what to do or say, hug us.

Please avoid saying:

- *I know your pain* … and compare it to anything but losing a child. Nothing is the same.

- *They are in a better place.* The best place is here.

- *Everything happens for a reason.* Maybe one day we will all have a better understanding of such matters, but no one knows that for a fact.

- *This too shall pass.* Grief lasts a lifetime; it is not the stomach flu.

- *Time heals all wounds.* No, it does not. We will grieve for a lifetime.

- *It was God's will or God needed another angel.* You can't possibly know this. We may believe our children are now angels, but please refrain from saying this.

- *Aren't you over it yet?* There is no timeline.

- *Be grateful you still have other children.* This removes any importance of our child's life. They were special and unique and cannot be replaced.

- *We are never given more than we can handle.* To us, this sounds like you are saying our loss is no big deal.

- *You're so strong/brave.* No one gave us a choice.

- *You're holding up so well.* What you see on the outside is not necessarily a reflection of what we are feeling on the inside.

- *Losing a child happens to lots of people.* This may be true but at this moment our world has fallen apart. Please do not minimize the fact that our child has died.

- *You're not your old self.* We will never be the person we once were. We are forever changed.

- *If there's anything I can do, call me.* We don't have the capacity to think through this. Instead, just do something. Anything thoughtful is perfect. Examples include: dropping off food or necessities like Kleenex and bathroom tissue, shovelling the driveway or stopping by for short visits.

- *You need to move on.* In time, we will learn how to move forward with our grief, but we will never "move on". This will happen when we are ready.

- *You have so much to be grateful for.* That may be true, but when we are struggling and missing our child, the other things in our lives do not balance out our missing child.

"All we really want is to never forget our child, to be able to say their name without causing others discomfort, and to be able to show them off to the world."

~ *Patti LeBlanc, mother of Michael born into heaven and Daniel, 24 years old*

Discussion Questions

These questions are meant to help you move further into your HEALING. You may want to answer these on your own or with a group. I also invite you to join the Journey to HEALING community at https://www.facebook.com/LisaKBoehmSupport.

Chapter 1 – The Journey Begins

1. What does the short story "The Suitcase" reveal about grief?
2. Does the metaphor of a suitcase ring true to your own experience? Why or why not?
3. Are you satisfied with your healing up to this point?
4. What fears do you have about exploring your own path to HEALING?

Chapter 2 – *Totally Unprepared*

1. Do you feel you are stuck in grief or are you beginning the journey to HEALING? Give examples.
2. Which path have you spent the most time with? The easy path that leads nowhere or the challenging path of HEALING? How are you feeling about your choice?
3. At times, do you feel you are the only one travelling this path? What steps can you take to feel more connected?

Chapter 3 – *Fork in the Road*

1. Have you let your grief define you? Or, have you chosen to live in spite of your loss? Give examples.
2. Have you worked through your pain? If you're still in the process, what actions and steps do you think you need to take?
3. Do you feel frightened to move forward? Why or why not?

Chapter 4 – *Trust your Compass*

1. What are your instincts telling you about HEALING?
2. Do you feel ready to choose your path to HEALING? Why or why not?
3. If you are not ready now, will you re-assess your readiness at a later time? Why or why not? What would have to change for you to be ready?

Chapter 5 – *healing vs HEALING*

1. Are you open to this new way of HEALING?
2. Up to this point, what steps have you found helpful?

3. Do you find other mothers' experiences helpful? Why or why not?

4. Do you agree that grief has no timeline? Have you felt pressure from yourself or others to 'hurry up'?

5. Grief is often considered something we deal with internally. Do you think you keep grief to yourself?

Chapter 6 – Honouring

1. In what ways have you honoured your child?

2. How does it make you feel when you do something in memory of your child?

3. Do you like to keep these activities or events private or do you like to share them with others?

4. Are there any special rituals of remembrance that you and your family do for your child's birthday or anniversary?

Chapter 7 – Exercise and Self-care

1. Do you agree that grief is felt physically? What physical ways has grief affected you?

2. Do you consider self-care an important factor in HEALING? Why or why not?

3. Do you have the support of your family to eat healthier? If not, are there other people in your life that can help you get on track and stay on track?

4. How can you make more time for exercise?

Chapter 8 – Assistance

1. Do you tend to isolate yourself from others? Why or why not?

2. Where have you looked for support? What resources are available in your community?

3. Have you reached out to other "angel moms"? Why or why not?

4. Have there been groups where you felt comfortable sharing your story? What was useful in this situation? What was not useful?

Chapter 9 – Living your Best Life

1. What would your child want you to be doing with your life? Why do you think that?

2. When was the last time you laughed (or even giggled)?

3. What was your favourite activity to do before your child died? Are you continuing to pursue this? Why or why not?

4. Who can help you live your best life?

Chapter 10 – Ideas and Intentions

1. Do you believe that your mindset plays a role in how you journey through HEALING? Why or why not?

2. Do you find yourself living with grief in one hand and love in the other? Give an example.

3. Do you have any mantras or positive self-talk phrases that you say to yourself when you are struggling?

4. How do you get through the darkest days of grief?

Chapter 11 – Nurturing your Soul

1. Do you find yourself gravitating more to traditional spirituality or do you seek solace through other spiritual means? Why?

2. Are you open to learning new ways to nurture your soul? Why or why not?

3. Have you researched spiritual books? Your local library is a good place to start.

4. Are there times when theological answers feel hurtful?

5. How has your belief (or lack thereof) in the afterlife shaped your grief?

Chapter 12 – Gratitude

1. What are three things you are grateful for right now?

2. Is there someone you sense needs forgiveness around the death of your child?

3. Do you have trouble thinking that gratitude is helpful on this journey? Why or why not?

Chapter 13 – Your Path

1. Do you feel your path now has more clarity? Why or why not?

2. Did you fill out the Check Points at the end of each chapter in the Map section? Why or why not? If you did, what will be your first step?

3. How do you hope to feel when you start your journey to HEALING?

4. Do you expect this path to be easy or hard or both? Explain.

Chapter 14 – Road under Construction

1. What might be a challenge or barrier for you to overcome on your path? What is one way you can change that?
2. What triggers do you experience? How can you work towards feeling more control over those triggers?
3. What are some new ideas for celebrating your child on their birthday or anniversary?

Chapter 15 – Take the Scenic Route

1. What's your favourite memory of your child?
2. How has your child's death changed you? Are you more empathetic? Kind? More likely to reach out? How does that make you feel?
3. What beauty and meaning have your found in your suitcase of grief?

Acknowledgements

Writing a book is not a solo act. Without these incredible people I would have given up a long time ago and this book would never have come to fruition. Thank you seems so inadequate. I appreciate and love you all.

Heartfelt thanks to:

Darryl – my dedicated and solid husband. You keep me upright when I start to fall.

Ryan – my 'why' – you gave me reasons to keep going when I didn't think I could. You have taught me so much.

Melanie Delorme – my supporter and mentor from day one.

Kary Oberbrunner – my coach and publisher. You believed in me before I did.

Samson – my furry friend and best writing partner.

My Beta Readers – Bob Boehm, Patrick Davis, Melanie Delorme, Alyson Melenchuk, Dr. Val Harding, Christalee Froese, and Marlene Jackson - my sounding board. Your feedback took this book to the next level.

Each and every mother who shared their children and their experience in this book – my trusted travel companions. I wish with all my heart that this path did not exist but I am grateful to walk it with you. It is my honour to make sure your children are never forgotten.

Notes

Chapter 2

1. Institute of Medicine (US) Committee on Palliative and End-of-Life Care for Children and Their Families. "Bereavement Experiences After the Death of a Child." *When Children Die: Improving Palliative and End-of-Life Care for Children and Their Families,* U.S. National Library of Medicine, 1 Jan. 1970, www.ncbi.nlm.nih.gov/books/NBK220798/.

2. "Kübler-Ross Model." *Wikipedia,* Wikimedia Foundation, 6 Sept. 2018, en.wikipedia.org/wiki/K%C3%BCbler-Ross_model.

3. Shermer, Michael. "Five Fallacies of Grief: Debunking Psychological Stages." *Scientific American,* 1 Nov. 2008, www.scientificamerican.com/article/five-fallacies-of-grief/.

Chapter 4

4. Froese, Christalee. *Journey to Joy: The Transformation of a life...21 Days at a Time.* (Regina, SK: Your Nickels Worth Publishing, 2018), 222

Chapter 5

5. Delorme, Melanie D. *After the Flowers Die: A Handbook of Heartache, Hope and Healing after Losing a Child.* (Powell, Ohio, Author Academy Elite, 2017). 66-67

6. "Tom Zuba. TomZuba.com LLC. 2018. Accessed July 5, 2018. Https://www.tomzuba.com/pages/toms-story/

7. Zuba, Tom. "Tom Zuba Teaches a New Way to Do Grief." Facebook. September 30, 2017. Accessed October 10, 2018. Http://www.facebook.com/tomzuba1

Chapter 6

8. Trudeau. Margaret. *Changing My Mind.* (Toronto: HarperCollins Canada, 2011), 253

9. Williams, Litza. "Worden's Four Tasks of Mourning." What's Your Grief? March 28, 2017. Accessed October 10, 2018. https://whatsyourgrief.com/wordens-four-tasks-of-mourning/.

10. Gilbert, Allison. "A Guide to Celebrating Deceased Loved Ones." CNN. April 12, 2016. Accessed July 9, 2018. https://www.cnn.com/2016/04/12/health/passed-present-projects-remember-deceased/index.html.

Chapter 7

11. Osmond, Marie, and Marcia Wilkie. *The Key Is Love: My Mothers Wisdom, a Daughter's Gratitude.* (New York City: New American Library, 2013). 146-147

12. Harvard Health Publishing. "Exercise Is an All-Natural Treatment to Fight Depression." Harvard Health. August 2013. Accessed July 25, 2018.

13. Cook, Gareth. "The Science of Healing Thoughts." Scientific American. January 19, 2016. Accessed July 14, 2018.https://www.scientificamerican.com/article/the-science-of-healing-thoughts/.

14. Westover, Arthur N., and Lauren B. Marangell. "A Cross-national Relationship between Sugar Consumption and Major Depression?" Depression and Anxiety. October 30, 2002. Accessed November 6, 2018. https://onlinelibrary.wiley.com/doi/abs/10.1002/da.10054.

15. Chatterjee, Dr. Rangan. "How Food Can Improve Your Mental Health." BBC News. May 22, 2017. Accesssed November 28, 2018. https://www.bbc.com/news/health-39976706.

16. Hall-Flavin, M.D. Daniel K. "Vitamin B-12 and Depression: Are They Related?" Mayo Clinic. June 01, 2018. Accessed August 06, 2018. https://www.mayoclinic.org/diseases-conditions/depression/expert-answers/vitamin-b12-and-depression/faq-20058077.

17. "Dehydration." Mayo Clinic. February 15, 2018. Accessed November 28, 2018. https://www.mayoclinic.org/diseases-conditions/dehydration/symptoms-causes/syc-20354086

18. Barkin, Carol and Ellen Mitchell. *Beyond Tears: Living after Losing a Child.* (New York: St. Martins Griffin), 2009.

Chapter 9

19. "Finding Joy After Loss." Psychology Today. April 2, 2013. Accessed July 19, 2018. https://www.psychologytoday.com/ca/blog/rethinking-mental-health/201304/finding-joy-after-loss.

Chapter 10

20. "Finding Light in the Darkness of Grief." Open to Hope. March 14, 2014. Accessed August 7, 2018. https://www.opentohope.com/finding-light-in-the-darkness-of-grief.

21. Lemoine, Eddie. *Bring about What You Think about.* (Bedford: Eddie Lemoine Consulting, 2010), 35

22. Gandhi, Mahatma. "A Quote by Mahatma Gandhi." Goodreads. 2018. Accessed November 7, 2018. https://www.goodreads.com/quotes/1163097-keep-your-thoughts-positive-because-your-thoughts-become-your-words.

23. Lipton, Bruce H. *The Biology of Belief: Unleashing the Power of Consciousness, Matter & Miracles.* Carlsbad, CA: Hay House, 2016. P. 144

Chapter 11

24. Hanish, Kiley. "My Journey with Yoga, Pregnancy Loss and the Road to Healing after Grief." SheKnows. October 27, 2015. Accessed August 18, 2018. https://www.sheknows.com/health-and-wellness/

articles/1100399/how-yoga-helped-me-grieve-after-losing-a-child.

25. Davis, Jeanie Lerche. "Can Prayer Heal?" WebMD. n.d. Accessed November 07, 2018. https://www.webmd.com/balance/features/can-prayer-heal.

26. "Healing After Loss: Meditation for Grieving." The Chopra Center. February 24, 2017. Accessed August 17, 2018. https://chopra.com/articles/healing-after-loss-meditation-for-grieving.

Chapter 12

27. Buckley, Kelly S. *Gratitude in Grief: Finding Daily Joy and a Life of Purpose following the Death of My Son.* (North Charleston, SC: CreateSpace Independent Publishing Platform, 2017), *x*, 61, 304

28. Greene, N., and K. McGovern. "Gratitude, Psychological Well-being, and Perceptions of Posttraumatic Growth in Adults Who Lost a Parent in Childhood." Death Studies. August 2017. Accessed July 31, 2018. https://www.ncbi.nlm.nih.gov/pubmed/28346066

29. "7 Scientifically Proven Benefits of Gratitude." Psychology Today. April 3, 2015. Accessed July 23, 2018. https://www.psychologytoday.com/us/blog/what-mentally-strong-people-don't-do/201504/7-scientifically-proven-beneftis-gratitude.

Chapter 13

30. Hinton, Clara. *Child Loss: The Heartbreak and the Hope.* (Shanksville, Pennsylvania. Clara Hinton, 2016), *ii,iii*, 83

Chapter 14

31. "Grief Triggers and Positive Memory: A Continuum." What's Your Grief? October 5, 2015. Accessed November 7, 2018. https://whatsyourgrief.com/grief-triggers-positive-memories-continuum/.

32. "The Definition of Insanity Is..." Psychology Today. July 27, 2009. Accessed August 13, 2018. https://www.psychologytoday.com/ca/blog/in-therapy/200907/the-definition-insanity-is.

33. "Frances Shand Kydd Quote." A-Z Quotes. Accessed July 21, 2018. https://www.azquotes.com/quote/665961.

Chapter 15

34. Davis, Danielle. "The Incredible Story of How a Mom Found Happiness After Losing A Child." Today's the Best Day. May 31, 2018. Accessed September 29, 2018. https://www.todaysthebestday.com/mom-found-happiness-after-losing-a-child/.

35. "Lao Tzu Quotes." BrainyQuote. Accessed November 07, 2018. https://www.brainyquote.com/quotes/lao_tzu_137141.

For more information about
the author or learn more about her online support community,
visit **www.LisaKBoehm.com**

Email: Lisa@LisaKBoehm.com

**Facebook: https://www.facebook.com/
LisaKBoehmSupport**